# Hope *in the* Midst *of* Depression

## Mary Southerland

HARVEST HOUSE PUBLISHERS

EUGENE, OREGON

Cover by Left Coast Design, Portland, Oregon

Cover photo © Richard Kolker / The Image Bank / Getty Images

HOPE IN THE MIDST OF DEPRESSION
Copyright © 2007 by Mary Southerland
Formerly titled *Coming Out of the Dark*
Copyright © 2004 by Mary Southerland

Published by Harvest House Publishers
Eugene, Oregon 97402
www.harvesthousepublishers.com

ISBN-13: 978-0-7369-1843-5
ISBN-10: 0-7369-1843-4

Library of Congress Cataloging-in-Publication Data

Southerland, Mary.
  Coming out of the dark / Mary Southerland.
    p. cm.
  ISBN 0-7369-1454-4
  1. Depressed persons—Religious life. 2. Depression, Mental—Religious aspects—Christianity. I.
Title.
  BV4910.34.S68 2004
  248.8'625—dc22                                                       2004001426

**Printed in the United States of America**

07  08  09  10  11  12  13  / VP-SK /  10  9  8  7  6  5  4  3  2  1

*This book is dedicated to those who dwell in the darkness
and have lost all hope. I pray this book will
guide you to the One who is Light
and the Giver of hope.*

*This book is dedicated to those who are helplessly
watching a loved one struggle against the darkness.
I pray this book will enable you to better understand
that struggle and equip you to help
the one you love.*

*This book is dedicated to those who have climbed
out of that pit! You are a trophy of God's power
and grace! I pray this book will affirm your journey and
allow you to help others on theirs.*

# ❊ Acknowledgments ❊

Thanks to my husband—Dan. You know me better than I know myself. Your love for me has defined who I am. Your willingness to take this journey with me is a priceless gift of unselfish love. You are my best friend and most constant cheerleader.

Thanks to my children—Jered and Danna. You have made me complete and filled my life with incredible joy and meaning. You are my greatest teachers.

Thanks to my friends—Michelle and Jay. You stepped into our lives and with a tenacious love walked through our darkest days. Jay, you encouraged and loved Dan when I couldn't. Michelle, you are my soul mate.

Thanks to my family—Betty and Carey. You helped me grow up. You are more than sister and brother-in-law. You are friends.

Thanks to the pastors and people of Flamingo Road. You stood with me in the darkness and prayed me to the light. You are the most precious church I know.

Thanks to all of the women who have encouraged me to write this book and refused to let me quit. I pray that I have told our story well.

Thanks to the One who began this good work in me—Jesus Christ. You are my Lord and Friend. You have never failed me nor forsaken me. Your love has formed me. Your delight in me is amazing. Please accept this book as an offering of praise for all that You have done in and through me! I love You.

# ✳ Contents ✳

# What *Am I* Doing *in This* Pit?

IT WAS THE SPRING OF 1995 and Spring Breakaway was just around the corner. Normally this event was the highlight of my year. I had always looked forward to teaching at this very special retreat for women in Fort Lauderdale, Florida. But not this year. This year I didn't even want to go, and I certainly did not want to teach.

I felt completely empty and totally drained. My energy was gone. My heart and mind seemed paralyzed. I was absolutely exhausted in every way. But then, I had a right to feel that way. After all, it had been a nonstop year for me.

My husband, Dan, was the pastor/teacher of Flamingo Road Church, a contemporary, seeker-sensitive ministry in Fort Lauderdale that had exploded in growth that year and begun meeting in multiple services. I attended every service, going early to welcome newcomers and staying late to smooth any ruffled feathers that came my way. We were in the process of transitioning from a very traditional church to a very contemporary one. Change is always hard, but this experience had been a nightmare. I had never encountered such opposition. I had never been the target of such criticism. I had never known such rejection as people I thought were my friends attacked my husband's integrity, heart, and vision. It seemed as if there was always someone waiting in line to question and criticize what we were doing. I felt like a walking wound. I knew we were being obedient to what God had called us to do, but it seemed that many disagreed. I was hurt and angry, and I did not know what to do with those emotions.

Music has always been an important part of my life. In the past, music had been a source of great joy and healing as well as a precious avenue of service. In hard times and in good times, I would sit down at the piano and sing it all out. But lately, I had grown to hate Tuesdays and Thursdays, the days when I taught 20 piano and voice students how to joyfully serve God with their musical gifts. I felt like a hypocrite. Now I, the teacher, found myself dreading going to church each weekend. My ministry as the church pianist had become more of a pain than a joy. Singing was no longer the overflow of a daughter's full heart, but the hollow performance of a spiritual chore.

I had been traveling a great deal, speaking at conferences and retreats for women. I directed the very active ladies' ministry of our church and taught a community Bible study each Tuesday morning. At least two or three times a week, I met with women in crisis who needed a listening ear, a caring heart, and a solution for the problems they were facing. It was only natural for these women to expect me to listen, to empathize, and to hand out answers filled with great wisdom because my husband was a pastor, and everyone knows a pastor's wife has her act together.

My son, Jered, was eleven and my daughter, Danna, was eight at the time. They kept me running with school and church activities, homework, soccer games, baseball practices, and the daily race of childhood. I had always loved being a mom, but, lately, even this role felt more like an unwelcome burden.

My house was spotless. It had to be. After all, a perfect woman has a perfect house. Since we lived in a neighborhood near our church, people dropping by was an everyday occurrence. We also hosted the new members' reception at our home each month as well as a Christmas open house for the entire church.

I was used to being the one who gave help. I was always the one others came to for strength and direction. I was the great encourager—the caregiver. People who knew me well would describe me as someone who was very strong. All of my life, I was driven to excel in everything, and if I couldn't do it perfectly, I didn't do it at all. I was a raging perfectionist...legalistically disciplined...with little sympathy for weak people. Now I, the strong one, couldn't get out of bed. The simplest decision sent me into a panic. The great wisdom-giver could not compile a grocery list. The woman who taught hundreds of women couldn't bring herself to face crowds of any size. The large tasks of life were out of the question, and even the simplest tasks seemed like huge mountains.

Meals, housework, and even shopping were all left undone. If I managed to get out of bed and get dressed by the time my kids got home from school, the day was a success. All I wanted to do was sleep and be left alone. I was paralyzed. I had fallen into a deep, dark, nameless pit. I had no idea how I got there. And even more frightening was the stark reality that I had no idea how to get out.

I decided I was just tired. All I needed was some rest. With that hope in hand, my family and I escaped the hot, humid flatlands of Florida to enjoy three weeks in the cool mountains of North Carolina, my favorite vacation spot. That vacation is a complete blur. I remember very little about our time there. My two responses, when asked any question during those three weeks, were "I don't know" and "I don't care." My children knew something was terribly wrong. They had never seen their mom so quiet…so still…and so sad. Dan listened patiently as I poured out my fear and confusion night after night. There seemed to be no answers…only questions. I could see the growing fear in his eyes that I felt in my own heart. We had never been here before. It was a foreign land. These were unfamiliar waters that we had no idea how to navigate. It was very simple. I was in serious trouble, and I needed help.

As each day grew darker, Dan and I both realized we had to come up with a plan—quickly! We decided I would see a Christian counselor Dan often referred people to and in whom he had great confidence. Her name was Betty Wells. My first visit with Betty was uneventful as far as I could tell…and a total waste of time. She did, however, accomplish one thing. She named my pit.

Clinical depression was a problem I knew little about. Evidently, it was an enemy that strong, committed Christians were not supposed to encounter, because I had never heard anyone in the church even talk about depression, much less admit they struggled with it. I recoiled at the thought of such blatant weakness in my life. I felt ashamed of what was obviously a great failure on my part, but I was very desperate and willing to do whatever it took to climb out of that pit. I also knew I could not make this journey alone. Over the next several months, Betty and Dan, along with many others, climbed down into that dark, slimy pit with me and became God with skin on. They sounded the alarm and gathered the troops.

Today, I can say with the certainty of an experienced pit dweller that there is a way out. I am not a psychologist. I am not a Bible scholar. I am just like many of you who are desperately seeking light and freedom from the darkness. I simply want to share my heart, my pain, my victory…and my journey out of my pit.

In the midst of those dismal days, God gently whispered fresh hope to my weak and wounded spirit. He nurtured it and grew it until that tiny sliver of hope became a sure and solid foundation upon which He has built a new life, a stronger life, a better life. God gave that hope to me in the darkness, but it has become an even more precious certainty in the light. This same certain hope can be yours today.

That hope is found in Psalm 40:1-3:

> I waited patiently for the LORD; he turned to me and heard my cry. He lifted me out of the slimy pit, out of the mud and mire; he set my feet on a rock and gave me a firm place to stand. He put a new song in my mouth, a hymn of praise to our God. Many will see and fear and put their trust in the LORD.

I have good news for you. I believe that one reason God allowed me to experience the pit of depression is to help others find the way out. I want to say to those of you who are in that pit—and to those of you who are peering over the edge of it wondering how to help someone you love—that you do not have to be a prisoner of the dark. You do not have to stay in your pit. You do not have to stand helplessly by while a friend or family member drowns in the darkness of depression. We were meant to dwell in the light. So lift up your head, open up your heart, and listen for the voice of the One who knows you best and loves you most. He can and will bring you out of the dark.

# 1

# Understanding Depression

FLORIDA IS FAMOUS FOR ITS SINKHOLES. Being born and raised in Texas, I find sinkholes fascinating. The ground suddenly collapses with no warning and seemingly for no reason. Actually, it is the culmination of a long process. Scientists say that sinkholes occur when underground resources dry up, causing the soil at the surface to lose its underlying support. Then everything simply caves in and an ugly pit is formed.

Depression and sinkholes have a lot in common. Depression seems to overwhelm with a vicious suddenness, but in reality it is a subtle and gradual process. Inner resources are slowly depleted until one day there is no energy of any kind to maintain normal activities. The world caves in and our existence seems to be swallowed up in the darkness of a black hole.

Many people believe depression is a spiritual problem. Others believe it is a physical problem. I believe it is both.

The world knows depression as a health problem. As a matter of fact, depression is America's number one health problem.

Studies indicate that as many as half of all women and one out of three men struggle with depression on a regular basis. I think we can safely say that almost everyone experiences depression at some point in life.

God is familiar with depression. He came to earth and was a man just like us. His ears are open to the cries of our hearts. In Psalm 40, David vividly describes depression as a pit. A slimy pit. A pit filled with mud and mire. It is the picture of a swamp where there is no stability...no solid ground. Escape seems impossible because there is nothing to hold on to. Fear reigns, wreaking havoc from its throne of incredible darkness and unspeakable loneliness. It takes someone who has experienced the tortuous reality of that pit to describe it in such personal ways.

Depression has been called a dark tunnel without a ray of light. Many cartoonists portray it as a little black cloud hovering overhead. I have a friend who once told me, "Some days you are the bug. Some days you are the windshield." But Psalm 42:6 says it best, "O my God, my soul is cast down within me" (NKJV).

I felt as if my soul had been ripped out of me, thrown on the ground, and trampled by a herd of angry elephants. It seemed as though I had been cast into a prison of unending darkness, a bottomless pit of pain filled with the numbing fear that this just might be the place where I would have to stay. The first step out of this dark pit is to face and understand depression for what it really is—an illness that permeates and affects every part of our identity.


## WHO STRUGGLES WITH DEPRESSION?

Before my personal experience in the pit, my two favorite spiritual encouragements to any Christian in trouble were "get over it" and "deal with it." My picture of the victorious Christian did not allow room for weakness. After all, I was a pastor's wife and teacher, a grounded Christian. People like me were not sup-posed to struggle with depression.

Remember who wrote Psalm 40? David—the man who had it all. As a young shepherd boy David killed the infamous giant, Goliath. He then went on to become a general, king, husband, father, and devoted follower of God. Success, money, power, and prestige were an accepted reality in his life. God described David as a man after His own heart. People like that should not struggle with depression. But David did—along with many other choice servants of God.

- Job longed for death and even questioned why he was ever born.

- Elijah sat under a juniper tree and begged God to let him die.

- The apostle Paul writes in his second letter to the Corinthians: "We were under great pressure, far beyond our ability to endure, so that we despaired even of life" (2 Corinthians 1:8).

- Martin Luther, a great man of God, wrote the ageless hymn "A Mighty Fortress Is Our God" from his own deep pit of depression.

- Charles Spurgeon was one of the greatest preachers to ever live. Yet he often battled depression.

- On the night before He was crucified, Jesus went to the Garden of Gethsemane to pray. Feeling completely abandoned and totally alone. I am certain He felt as if He had fallen into a deep, dark pit from which there was no escape. On the cross He cried out, in all of His humanity, to His Father because He, like you and me, felt such pain and sorrow.

So cheer up. If you struggle with depression, you are in great company. Who struggles with depression? The answer is very simple: Anyone can.

## WHAT FACTORS LEAD TO DEPRESSION?

There are many factors that can trigger or lead to depression. Because I am not an expert in the medical or psychological world, I will just share with you the major factors I experienced in my life.

### Lack of Replenishing Relationships

The pit of depression is a place of isolation. It is a place where relationships have been ignored, mishandled, or poorly developed. There are three kinds of relationships in our lives.

> *Emotional health is like a bank account; the withdrawals and deposits determine the balance.*

**Replenishing relationships.** Replenishing relationships are those relationships that give back, making your life fuller and richer. They restore and refresh you. When life deflates you, replenishing people pump you back up.

**Neutral relationships.** Colorless and vague, neutral relationships are merely present in your life. They do not replenish or even deplete, but they do take up valuable emotional room.

**Draining relationships.** Draining relationships literally suck the life out of you, exhausting and depleting valuable emotional resources. I call these people emotional black holes because it really doesn't matter how much time or energy you give them.

Regardless of how much of yourself you invest in them, it will never be enough.

Emotional health is like a bank account; the withdrawals and deposits determine the balance. We get out of balance when we make too many withdrawals and not enough deposits. When we do not pursue replenishing relationships and we continually throw ourselves and our limited emotional resources away in one emotional black hole after another, we will soon find ourselves emotionally bankrupt.

It is very easy to become emotionally overdrawn and overspent. Many times, we are so busy with life that we lose sight of the basic truth that our most important replenishing relationship grows from the intimacy which we were created to enjoy in Jesus Christ. In other words, I had become so wrapped up in His work that I had failed to be wrapped up in His presence.

## Poor Self-Image

Psalm 40:2 says that the pit of depression is filled with mud, causing us to have an unclear or dirty picture of who we are.

I had spent my whole life trying to earn God's favor, trying to prove my worth. I had desperately hoped to make Him and everyone else in my life love me because of my performance. That faulty understanding led to wrong priorities, unrealistic expectations, a constant practice of self-condemnation, and a whole lot of stress. I soon discovered there was a very large "S" tattooed on my chest. I was struggling, with every breath, to be Superwoman—all things to all people.

Many times we try to serve Him with gifts we do not have. During my "pit experience," I learned an important truth: God gives us everything we need to accomplish what He created us to do. When we step out of that empowerment, we are stepping into our own strength, depending upon our own resources. Those resources are very limited. Our human strength will soon be depleted and the pit of burnout and depression is just around the corner.

## Past Experiences

Like David, we carefully pack away old hurts, unconfessed sins, and denied pain, hoping it will all simply disappear. Instead, this emotional baggage David calls "mire" becomes a malignant source of decay and destruction.

We used to live in South Florida, which is famous for its beautiful beaches. When my children were small, we would pack the car with a picnic lunch and head for the water. One of their favorite games was to see which one could hold a beach ball under the water for the longest time.

They would wade out into the ocean, push the ball under the water, and begin to count. Soon their arms would tire, or the beach ball would escape their control and pop up to the surface. This is exactly what happens to the "mire" in our lives. It settles at the bottom of our souls, popping up every once in a while until we finally run out of energy to keep it submerged. It then works its way to the surface and spills its ugliness and darkness over every part of our existence. "Mire" comes in all shapes and sizes:

- pain that has never been faced
- anger that has been left unresolved
- sin we refuse to deal with
- a great loss
- the death of a dream
- the death of a loved one

My father died when I was four years old. My mother was

forced to sell the farm my dad had spent a lifetime building and move to the small nearby town of Brownwood, Texas. She worked as a waitress at night while attending nursing school during the day. Even after she became a licensed vocational nurse, she was still forced to babysit and clean houses in order to support my brother, my sister, my grandmother, and myself. When I was five years old, Mama began a 25-year battle with cancer. That battle overshadowed everything else in my childhood. There was little communication in my family because there simply wasn't time or energy. Feelings were not shared; they were stuffed down, out of sight. The "mire" of my life began to settle at a very young age, and I had not even realized it was there.

> *When you bury pain alive, it keeps*
> *popping up at unexpected moments.*

When I went to see my counselor for the first time, she asked me to write down some of my early childhood memories. She handed me a spiral notebook with firm instructions to "keep it simple," encouraging me not to think about those days too much, but to just write what came to my mind. It took a week to complete what I perceived to be a totally useless assignment. To my surprise, when she asked me to read aloud what I had written, an unsettling pattern emerged. Nineteen out of the 20 memories were negative. I had never really acknowledged or faced most of them. Other painful memories were there, lurking in the unsurrendered and unexposed corners of my heart, waiting for me to deal with them. Some I had hidden away because they just hurt too much.

In the weeks that followed, the Lord and I sifted through the enormous pile of "mire" that had settled into my spirit and life. Together we faced experiences I had carefully locked away until they slammed into my heart and mind with breathtaking pain. An alcoholic father. A family doctor and friend who had molested me during a visit to his office. Times of loneliness and rejection. Failures that had haunted me. Conversations filled with hurt. Unreasonable fears that were never spoken. It seemed as if the flood of memories would never end.

But God is good. I believe He gives us a defense mechanism for those experiences that are beyond our ability to face. He gently tucks them away until He brings us to the place where we are able to deal with them. As I faced the truth of my childhood memories, I gained a sense of strength and purpose. God had not allowed those experiences to touch my life without a reason. I began to feel a new appreciation for my mother. I realized what a wonderful and strong woman she was. I understood that she loved me with all of her heart. I now know that every ounce of her strength had to be poured into sheer survival. She did the best she could. Facing the truth had not been easy, but it had resulted in good.

When you bury pain alive, it keeps popping up at unexpected moments. It must be dealt with and then buried…dead. We must deal with our past. We must screen every experience until we grasp its seed of victory. The will of God admits no defeat. The will of God penalizes no one. We can allow our past to defeat us or we can choose to harness that past and use it for power today. Painful experiences we try so hard to hide can be changed from the quicksand of defeat into stepping-stones of victory and healing.

## Lack of a Solid Foundation

In Psalm 40:2 David proclaims, "He set my feet on a rock and gave me a firm place to stand." This verse indicates that there had been no solid foundations in David's life. Or if there had been, someone or something had destroyed them. For whatever reason, he had no rock or firm place on which to stand.

Some of us are given a solid and stable foundation for life from childhood. Others are not. Some of us, by sheer tenacity, have carved this foundation out of our adulthood. Many have not and cannot.

What really matters more than the way you were or the way you are is the way you can be. Every day, with every experience, we must be growing into a life of balance. Luke 2:52 tells us that "Jesus grew in wisdom and stature, and in favor with God and men." As long as Jesus lived on earth, He continued to grow mentally, emotionally, physically, socially, and spiritually. In other words, He modeled the truth that the foundation for health in every area of life is balance. When our lives are out of control and unbalanced, we are an easy target for depression.

## A Final Thought

Before we can overcome our depression or help others to find a way out of their darkness, we must understand what depression is, who struggles with it, and identify the factors that can lead to depression. It is good to gain all the understanding we can about what causes depression. However, many people become so hung up trying to pinpoint every minor factor that they never reach a solution.

There has to be a way out of this pit...

# 2

# Climbing Out
## *of the* Pit

CHILDREN ARE WONDERFULLY DIFFERENT. When my son, Jered, was nine months old, he began to pull himself up on every piece of furniture that would hold his stocky frame. For weeks he maneuvered his way around our home until the day he took his first step...alone. Now, it was a step of only inches, but we all celebrated as if he had run a ten-mile race. And then there is my daughter, Danna, who crawled when she was four months old, before she could even sit up. We assumed she would be walking within a matter of weeks. Danna had a different plan. She never pulled herself up on a single piece of furniture. She never took a step. But one day, when she was ten months old, she stood up and ran across the room. Today Jered and Danna both walk extremely well as teenagers, but they each began with tiny steps and a plan uniquely their own.

Nobody becomes depressed overnight. Nobody overcomes it overnight. The journey out of the pit of depression is a process of steps uniquely planned by your Father. He is the Guide for your journey out of the darkness.

## STEP ONE: WAIT FOR GOD

In Psalm 40:1, David writes, "I waited patiently for the LORD." I had always thought of waiting as passive and considered it to be of little value, even a waste. But I began to see that waiting is active and can be a powerful spiritual experience.

### To Wait Means to Accept the Pit

When we commit our lives to God, nothing touches us that doesn't first pass through His hands. And as a painful experience passes through those hands of love, those hands that are committed to our growth, that painful experience is transformed. What once was destructive becomes a tool in the hands of our loving Father, who will take it, put a handle on it, and then use it as a tool for our good.

> *He loves us too much to
> waste our pain.*

When hard times come, we immediately begin to beg and bargain for rescue, for a way of escape. He loves us too much to waste our pain. He is more committed to our long-term maturity than our short-term comfort.

It is a shallow love that always rescues easily. It is a depthless love that always rescues quickly. Sometimes our Father says wait. So be patient, accept your pit, and know that He is at work.

This is really hard for me, because I hate to wait. After I had seen my counselor several times, I came home absolutely furious. I walked through the front door, slammed it behind me, and loudly announced to my husband, "I am not going back. She hasn't fixed anything."

Picture falling into a slimy pit. Your first reaction, like mine, would probably be to frantically claw and struggle and fight your way out. Then, when you have used up all of your energy, you stop struggling and sit down to rest and wait for help because that is all you can do. You have no other options.

When we come to the end of ourselves, then God begins His work of healing and restoration. But first we must learn to accept the pit and to wait. Part of waiting involves seeking. To wait on God is to seek Him, to examine every circumstance in search of His fingerprints. Waiting is trusting. Waiting is resting. Waiting is the absolute confidence that God will intervene. That choice to wait demands trust on our part because acceptance grows from the fertile soil of trust.

## To Wait Means to Admit There Is a Problem

We can be so proud and so self-sufficient. Admitting we are helpless and must wait on God is sometimes hard. In reality, we can learn to celebrate our helplessness. We can grow to the place of rejoicing in our weakness. Our weakness and helplessness are an invitation for the power of God to take up residence and display itself in our lives. Isaiah tells us that "He gives power to those who are tired and worn out; He offers strength to the weak" (Isaiah 40:29 NLT).

Steve Brown, a Christian author with a quick sense of humor, tells the story of three men who died and went to hell. The first man had served as a deacon, teacher, and leader in his church on earth. He was there every time the doors were open, but it was all just a show. He had merely been playing games with God. Now it was too late. The second man was searching everywhere for all of those hypocrites he had so often criticized in their religious zeal. They were not there. Maybe they had been right after all. How he wished he had listened to them. The third man was a widely known teacher of the principles of positive thinking. He was sitting in the corner with his head in his hands, repeating over and over again, "It's not hot and I'm not here."

Instead of hiding or trying to rationalize the darkness away, we must be willing to honestly admit that we are struggling with depression. Pride always hinders authenticity. Emotional health begins at the point of emotional integrity, when we can be truthful enough to say to ourselves and to others "I need help." We cannot be right until we choose to be real.

### To Wait Means to Practice Transparency

At this time my husband was the pastor/teacher of a large, very visible, and fast-growing church. Dan and I had a choice to make. We could choose to be transparent and real or we could attempt to claim our right to privacy and hide my struggle. We chose transparency and began to share our pain with the team God had assembled around us. The pastors and their wives were told in great detail. Our deacons, who are wonderful encouraging servants, were gathered together and told. Then we took an even bigger risk by sharing my struggle with the entire church.

We quickly discovered that sharing the crisis lessened its grip on our lives. The response to our transparency and willingness to share our pain with those who had known great pain themselves was absolutely overwhelming. People began to pray. Cards, letters, and Scripture verses came pouring through the mail. Women would show up at the front door with meals. At times, others came to clean my house, do my laundry, and entertain my children. Deacons would station themselves at various places in the church building during any worship service that I attended. If I were caught in a difficult situation or detained too long with someone, all I had to do was turn and nod to them. They would come, take me by the arm, and walk me to my car with a hug and instructions to go home.

Out of this transparency came another blessing, a precious gift of friendship. As Dan and I began to share what we were going through with others, a good friend, Michelle Johnson, stepped into my life. Because we needed a study at home, Dan and I had just moved to a house in the neighborhood where Michelle lived with her family. Michelle and I had known each other for several years because our children attended the same school and we had worked together in the women's ministry of our church.

One Tuesday morning I sat down with Michelle and explained that I would have to step out of all church leadership while working through my depression. Her response was immediate and strong. How could she help? What could she do? I did not even know what to tell her. It didn't matter. She just knew. Over the next few years, Michelle was always there. Time after time she stepped into situations and shielded me, protected me, loved me, and encouraged me. God used her friendship to save my life. Her husband Jay was a tremendous source of strength and encouragement to Dan, and our children became great friends. I have often wondered if my family and I would have missed this priceless gift of friendship had we chosen to handle my pain in private.

We were created to share our burdens with each other. Isaiah 35:3-4 is a clear directive: "Make the weak hands strong and the weak knees steady. Say to people who are frightened, 'Be strong. Don't be afraid. Look, your God will come, and he will punish your enemies. He will make them pay for the wrongs they did, but he will save you'" (NCV). We need each other. A shared load is a lighter load. Transparency brings healing. Authenticity yields restoration.

## To Wait Means to Embrace Solitude

In the pit it is so dark we cannot see. All we can do is wait and trust and rest. In the midst of my depression, I began to discover that darkness is a great place for solitude. Distractions are few. When the Light comes, it is easier to see. There are times when the silence makes His voice clear and strong.

"Be still, and know that I am God" (Psalm 46:10). We cannot know God on the run. Solitude lets our souls catch up.

In the jungles of Africa, a tourist was taking a safari. He hired natives from a tribe to carry all of the necessary supplies. On the first day, they walked rapidly and went far. The tourist was excited because he wanted to get there quickly. On the second morning, the tourist woke up early and ready to go, but the natives refused to move. They just sat and rested. When the tourist questioned them, he was told that they had gone too fast the first day. Now they were waiting for their souls to catch up.

What a profound concept they had grasped! Stress, hurry, and intense activity can cause us to lose our perspective, to disconnect from ourselves and from our purpose in life. The busier we are, the more we need regular solitude. I love the Greek motto that says: "You will break the bow if you keep it always bent." I broke. One of the main reasons I broke was that solitude had never been a part of my life. I was too busy being spiritual. I was too busy trying to earn God's love and approval. I was too busy trying to be good enough. I was too busy running from the past.

During my two years in the pit, I gave up every role of leadership in order to spend time in solitude, seeking God. It felt as though I were giving up my whole identity because so much of who I was had been built upon what I did. Many times I walked to the front door of our church, stopped, and had to walk away in panic. I just could not make myself go in. As I struggled with the guilt and self-condemnation of my frailty, the Father taught me an important truth that has revolutionized my life. He is more concerned with who I am than what I do. He loves me—warts and all. If I never do another thing in the kingdom, He still loves me. What I do or don't do does not affect His love for me. He simply loves me. That life-changing truth was born out of darkness—in solitude.

The first step out of the pit is to wait. While we wait we must admit there is a problem, accept the pit, practice transparency, and embrace solitude.

## Step Two: Cry Out for Help

"He turned to me and heard my cry" (Psalm 40:1).

Many times people in the prison of depression look for help in the wrong places. Let me share with you some of the right places to find help.

### Turn to God

Here's an amazing thought: The God of the universe, the One who created the world and flung the stars into space, waits and listens for the cry of His children. When they cry out, He comes to them just as a mother runs to her sick child, calling through the darkness of the night. God comes to us in many ways.

**Reading His Word.** "Your word is a lamp to my feet and a light for my path" (Psalm 119:105). I lived in the book of Psalms during the two darkest years of depression. I could no longer study, but I could meditate. A friend had given me an instrumental tape of hymns. Every day, I would plug in that tape, take the phone off of the hook, and read psalm after psalm. They were like water to a thirsty heart, an oasis to a weary child, for one wandering in a dry and barren desert. I found myself in the words I read and took great comfort in the fact that God was totally aware of everything I was feeling.

**Talking with Him.** "For the eyes of the LORD are on the righteous, and His ears are open to their prayers" (1 Peter 3:12 NKJV). The darkness called forth the most childlike prayers of my life. Day after day, night after night, I poured out the questions I had always been afraid to ask. I poured out my deepest fears and greatest pain. Those were the most honest and powerful prayers of my life.

I learned how to approach my Father with confidence, but I also learned how to listen as I had never listened before. I began to fall in love with the One who created me in my mother's womb and set me apart for Himself. When you spend time with Him, you will love Him and learn to know the sound of His voice.

**Writing to Him.** "Let love and faithfulness never leave you; bind them around your neck, write them on the tablet of your heart" (Proverbs 3:3). I began to journal. This habit became a dramatic part of my healing. I now know why God chose to reveal Himself in written form. It is powerful. Some days I wrote only a sentence or two. Other days I filled pages with discovered truths or unanswered questions. As I began to see Him work, the journal became a record of spiritual markers that were a constant reminder of His faithfulness to me even when I was faithless.

*Many times depression is rooted in a physical problem and may respond to medication.*

God is waiting for your invitation. He is listening for your voice. Right now, right where you are, cry out to Him for help.

*Turn to Doctors and Counselors*

Many people say depression is only a spiritual problem and

there are, therefore, only spiritual solutions for it. I could not disagree more.

I heard a story about a little girl who became frightened during a terrible storm. The little girl was so frightened that she cried out in fear. Her daddy came running, gathered her up in his arms, and held her tightly. As he held her, he explained she had nothing to fear because God would take care of her. The little girl thought for a moment and then replied, "I know God will take care of me and love me, but right now, Daddy, I need someone with skin on."

We often need "someone with skin on" to help us out of our depression. That person may be a physician. I encourage anyone experiencing depression to get a physical as soon as possible. Many times depression is rooted in a physical problem and may respond to medication. After a physical and several blood tests, my doctor discovered I had a chemical imbalance that had probably been present from early childhood. This chemical imbalance made me more prone to depression. I just thought that everyone saw life the way I saw it—like a poorly developed photograph black around the edges. It seemed as if I had lived my whole life trying to escape one dark shadow after another. I had no idea that a physical problem was contributing to my dark view of life. The doctor prescribed medication that would correct the imbalance, but it would not eliminate the depression. It simply enabled me to have the strength and energy to begin to deal with the issues that had led me to the pit. The medication leveled the playing field for me so that I could begin to deal with the multiple causes of my depression.

Christian counseling is another valuable weapon in the battle against depression. God gave counselors their gifts to use for Him in ministry. He must have known that we would need them. Betty Wells and Jim Vigorritto, the counselors who walked me through my crisis, have the gift of healing. They have balanced the psychological world with Scripture and the healing power of a living God. He used them as vital instruments of healing in my life. "Plans go wrong for lack of advice; many counselors bring success" (Proverbs 15:22 NLT).

## Turn to Your Support Team

A support team is essential for anyone in the pit of depression. My team carried me when I couldn't take another step. They loved me when I was unlovable. They encouraged me when I felt like giving up. I would still be in the darkness today if it weren't for my family, my church, and my friends.

When I married into the Southerland family, I didn't know that tent camping was part of the deal. I might have reconsidered (just kidding). I decided I could learn to camp and maybe even enjoy it. My first trip to Lake Greason in the foothills of the Ozarks was quite an experience. It didn't take me long to learn the routine.

Every day, my mother-in-law would prepare a huge breakfast. Afterward, the kids did dishes while Mom headed for her tent, where she changed into her swimsuit, put on her sunglasses, grabbed a towel, and headed for the lake. On the shore, she would select an inner tube, position her towel in a certain spot, wade into the water, and sit down in the tube. Then she would float blissfully for hours.

There was a slight problem with this plan. Lake Greason had a current that would carry Mom down the lake, around the bend, and into the path of ski boats. Several times a day, someone would have to swim after her, pulling her back to the safety of the shore, where she would profusely thank them and go right back to floating. Finally, the kids came up with a great idea. They grabbed a ski rope, tied one end to Mom's inner tube and the other end to a wooden stake driven securely into the ground on the shore. She could then float until the rope ran out and someone reeled her in.

This is exactly what the people on my support team did for me. They rescued me over and over again. They could see the dangers I was too weak to see. They loaned me their energy when mine was gone. They became a lifeline that kept me from drifting toward the brink of disaster. Did my depression affect their opinion of me? Absolutely. It showed them that I was just like them. I was not Superwoman. It gave them permission to face their own weaknesses. It modeled authenticity and transparency for them, and encouraged them to be real. I have taught many biblical truths in our church, but this truth was lived before them and is probably the most powerful lesson I have ever shared. We must cry out for help.

Some of you may be thinking that there is absolutely no one who will sign up to be a member of your support team. If you will cry out to God and honestly seek help, He will bring your helpers.

## STEP THREE: COUNT ON GOD

"He lifted me out of the slimy pit, out of the mud and mire; he set my feet on a rock and gave me a firm place to stand. He put a new song in my mouth, a hymn of praise to our God. Many will see and fear and put their trust in the LORD" (Psalm 40:2-3). This passage promises that He will free you. He will direct you. He will restore you. He will give you joy. He will use you to bring others to Himself.

That is quite an impressive to-do list when you are sitting at the bottom of an ugly pit, with the shattered pieces of your life scattered around you. But God's ways are not our ways. "Oh, what a wonderful God we have! How great are his riches and wisdom and knowledge! How impossible it is for us to understand his decisions and his methods!" (Romans 11:33 NLT).

God is drawn to brokenness. He turns first to the broken. Psalm 40:1 says, "he turned to me." Notice that it does not say David turned to God. I don't think David could. Knowing the desire of David's heart and understanding his weakness, God heard his cry and turned to David the same way He will hear your cry and turn to you. "Then they cried to the LORD in their trouble, and he saved them from their distress. He brought them out of darkness and the deepest gloom and broke away their chains" (Psalm 107:13-14). "I will lead the blind by ways they have not known, along unfamiliar paths I will guide them; I will turn the darkness into light before them and make the rough places smooth. These are the things I will do; I will not forsake them" (Isaiah 42:16).

During the darkest hours, I questioned God continually. I flung my anger at Him like a spear. My heart and soul were filled with fear and confusion instead of faith and trust. Yet He never turned away from me. He knew every tear that I cried. "You keep track of all my sorrows. You have collected all my tears in your bottle. You have recorded every one in your book" (Psalm 56:8 NLT).

Out of those tears and brokenness has come the most effective and powerful ministry of my life. I have discovered that the more we are broken, the more we are used. You can count on God. You can credit His grace to your account.

Mercy is when we don't get what we deserve. Justice is when we get what we do deserve. Grace is when we get what we do not deserve.

We are trophies of God's grace, and we can count on Him.

## STEP FOUR: DON'T GIVE UP

"I waited patiently for the LORD" (Psalm 40:1). Patience requires perseverance and tireless commitment. Be patient with yourself. Don't give up on you. Your journey is a marathon, not a 50-yard dash. On my journey, it took me 45 years to hit rock bottom. It has taken me four years to climb out…this far. I am still climbing. We must be patient. We must be willing to persevere.

This poem has helped me to understand the value of patience.

Two frogs fell into a can of cream,
Or so I've heard it told.
The sides of the can were shiny and steep,
The cream was deep and cold.

"Oh, what the use?" said No. 1.
"'Tis fate—no help's around.
Goodbye, my friend. Goodbye, sad world."
And weeping still, he drowned.

But No. 2, of sterner stuff,
Dog-paddled in surprise,
The while he wiped his creamy face,
And dried his creamy eyes.

*I'll swim a bit, at least,* he thought.
Or so I've heard it said.
*It wouldn't really help the world*
*If one more frog were dead.*

An hour or two he kicked and swam.
Not once he stopped to mutter.
But kicked and swam, and swam and kicked.
Then hopped out, via butter.*

Be patient. Keep kicking and swimming through the stuff that threatens to drown you. Patience and perseverance will pay off.

---

* Author unknown.

Years ago in a large southeastern city, the great pianist Paderewski was scheduled to perform. The city was alive with excitement, and the day finally came. In the crowd at the great concert hall that evening was a young mother clutching the hand of her small son. Hoping to inspire him to practice, she had brought him to hear the master perform. As they sat and waited for the concert to begin, she turned her head to look at the people as they filled the auditorium. The little boy saw his chance to escape. He quietly slipped from his seat and walked down the aisle toward the stage. Just as he reached the orchestra pit, a spotlight hit the grand piano and he gasped at the beauty of the instrument. No one noticed the little boy as he slipped up the side stairs to the stage and climbed up on the piano stool. No one noticed him at all, until he began to play "Chopsticks." The concert hall suddenly fell silent. Then people began to shout, "Get him off the stage." Backstage, Paderewski realized what had happened, grabbed his coat, and rushed to the little boy's side. Without a word, he bent down behind the little boy, placed his hands on either side of the boy's hands, and began to compose a beautiful countermelody to "Chopsticks." As they played together, he whispered in the little boy's ear, "Don't stop. Keep on. Don't quit."

The apostle Paul says it this way in Philippians 1:6, "And I am sure that God who began the good work within you will keep right on helping you grow in his grace until his task within you is finally finished on that day when Jesus Christ returns."

Right now...right where you are...your Father is standing beside you with His arms wrapped around you. Listen as He gently speaks, "Don't stop. Keep on. Don't quit."

Don't give up. Just give in and allow God to take control. He will turn that pit into an altar on which your broken spirit can be laid as a sweet sacrifice of praise. God wants you to experience restoration and then to be a vessel of restoration for others.

I know the music of your soul may be filled with chaos and dissonance, but even now, the Master is composing the rest of your song. And one day very soon, it will be a song of beauty and light. One day, you will come out of the dark.

# 3

# Getting Past
## *Your* Past

WHEN WE THINK OF THE PAST, some of us remember days when everything was better, simpler, and cheaper. For others, the past holds glittering images of satisfying accomplishments, successful achievements, and times of happiness. For still others, the past is something we would like to totally erase. We keep hoping for a giant bottle of white out to come along and magically blot out the pain. The past probably holds a little of all these things for each of us.

Someone once said, "Memory can be a wonderful treasure chest for those who know how to pack it." James Barrie wrote, "God gave us memories so that we might have roses in December."

Each one of us must deal with our past. Somehow we have to make the past our friend instead of our enemy. If we want victory today, hope for tomorrow, and lives that are free and filled with joy, then we must deal with our past for one very simple reason:

Our past is unchangeable. And though we cannot change our past, we can change our responses to it.

When my daughter, Danna, was a little girl I soon realized she was very much like me, particularly in her approach to mornings. I hate mornings, and so does Danna. I was always trying to entice her out of bed with breakfast. I soon learned that my best weapon of bribery was Cap'n Crunch's Peanut Butter Crunch cereal.

One morning Danna was moving very slowly, and I was growing very impatient. I called her to come eat her cereal as I poured it into the bowl. I was adding the milk when I heard her voice from the bedroom. "Mom, don't pour the milk in yet." Well, it was too late, but I thought to myself, "It won't hurt. She'll never know." When she walked into the kitchen a few minutes later, she took one look at the cereal, placed her hands on the spot where her hips would one day be, and, turning her pretty little button nose up in the air, announced, "I cannot eat that stuff." At that moment I wondered, "Whose idea was it to have kids?" Fortunately, it was just a fleeting thought. I calmly asked, "And just what is wrong with this cereal?" She looked at me with pity for someone so ignorant on the finer qualities of cereal cuisine and explained, "Mama, when you pour the milk too early Captain Cwunch gets soggy. And everybody knows that you can't get the cwunch back in it."

How do we recrunch our past? For the answer to that question I turn to one of my favorite people in the Bible, David. Now, here is a guy with a past. His story is found in the Old Testament books of 1 and 2 Samuel. David got caught in the trap of adultery. I know what you are thinking. A lot of people make that mistake. But David was not just anybody. His résumé is one that would impress anyone. More importantly, the Bible tells us that David was really special to God. He loved God and truly wanted to please Him. Men like that aren't supposed to commit adultery because they are smart enough and disciplined enough to avoid such common traps.

You are probably familiar with his story. David sent his soldiers into battle while he stayed home. Not a good plan. One day, David spotted a beautiful woman next door while she was taking a bath. All of his wisdom and discipline crumbled away in a moment. His heart for God was paralyzed by his own sinful desire, and David slept with Bathsheba. If that wasn't bad enough, he then sent her husband to the front lines where he was killed. David and Bathsheba began living together. They had children and tried to pretend everything was wonderful. But inside, David was dying. Psalm 32 tells us that he lost weight. He groaned under the weight of his sin. The pain of his betrayal was a constant companion. He hurt. He was always tired. Then God told on him, and everyone found out exactly what David had done. His life began to fall apart before him. People didn't trust him anymore. One child died, and two others were in serious trouble. His own son turned against him, pushing him off the throne so that he could take over. Soon after, this son was killed.

David cried out to God. He had finally come to the end of himself and was forced to face the ugly reality of his sin. He then confessed to everyone who was involved. God forgave David. He restored him to health and gave him back his throne. David lost some things forever, but restoration came to his life. And after all of this, God describes David as a man after His own heart (see 1 Samuel 13:14).

Why did God restore David? Because God is drawn to broken people. God loves to use broken people. The desire of God's heart is never condemnation; it is always restoration. David experienced the forgiving grace of God and discovered how to harness his yesterdays and make them a power in his life. David's life holds six truths that teach us how to get past the past.

## First Truth: Remember the Victories

How quickly we forget. The wonder of God working in our lives can become too familiar. The victories seem to be swallowed up by the defeats. David stopped and remembered the victories of his past—Goliath falling at his feet, the crown being placed on his head, battles he had won. As he relived those moments, the faithfulness and forgiving love of God washed over him and he gave thanks. In Psalm 107:1-2 he writes, "Oh, give thanks to the Lord, for He is good! For His mercy endures forever. Let the redeemed of the Lord say so" (nkjv).

*We need to keep victory journals.*

David then looks back over his life. He remembers the victories, whether they were great or small, and gives thanks. He urges us to join him in praising God, to remember all that God has done. He goes on in Psalm 108:1 to proclaim, "O God, my heart is fixed; I will sing and give praise" (kjv). A "fixed" heart is a determined heart, a focused heart, a steadfast heart. It is a heart that has gone back over the books and audited the work of God. We need to keep victory journals. We need to record the spiritual markers of our lives.

My family loves to vacation in North Carolina, and we particularly enjoy hiking or an occasional climb up a small mountain. On one such trip we visited Grandfather Mountain. My son, Jered, was nine years old and my daughter, Danna, was six. Grandfather Mountain has a swinging bridge you can cross for a breathtaking view, which we did. After visiting the gift shop, we decided to hike a quick trail. As we approached the starting point of the trail, I noticed a large sign warning all hikers to make sure that they were dressed properly and had plenty of snacks, water, and the correct hiking gear. When I pointed out this sign to my husband, he looked at me with surprise and said that it did not apply to Southerlands. I should have known.

The first hour was a nice, easy climb. Then we came to a fork in the path. We were standing there, wondering which way to go, when a group of college students came down, laughing and obviously enjoying themselves. We asked them which path we should take, pointing out that our children were small and wearing slip-on sneakers, and we were without a drop of water or one morsel of food. They said that the path they had just climbed would be perfect. (If I could find them today, they would be in serious trouble.)

Off we went. The first 15 minutes were great. Then the path grew more steep and treacherous, winding around sharp cliffs and over huge rocks. The children began to tire and stumble, and I began to wonder why I had ever married this man. At one point we rounded a corner to come face-to-face with the biggest boulder I had ever seen. I told Dan I could not go on. He looked at me and said, "You have to. You cannot go back down. This trail is the only way out, and it leads over the mountain." For the next two hours, we each held the hands of our children, carefully placing their feet so that they would not fall. I was not having fun. Finally, we came to the last boulder. When I saw it, I felt like dancing. There were wooden stakes bolted into the rock, creating a ladder. Someone had gone before us and made a way over the mountain.

The victories of yesterday can be the stakes in the mountains of today. God has gone before us and made a way. He made a way over the mountains and through the valleys of yesterday, and He will do it again. Hebrews 13:8 promises that "Jesus Christ is the same yesterday and today and forever." Remember the victories.

## SECOND TRUTH: CONFRONT THE DEFEATS

The will of God does not entertain defeat. God doesn't waste any experience in our lives. Some experiences come by His design, some come as consequences of our actions, but all come with His permission, filtered through His fingers of love.

One summer we were vacationing in North Carolina...again. The children wanted to go gem mining. Gem mining is a delightful experience. You pay an enormous amount of money and are presented with a rusty wooden tray that has a wirescreened bottom. Then you sit down in front of a wooden trough filled with orange, muddy water. As the water rushes through the trough, you dip your tray into the water and watch it spill over onto your shoes and clothes. When you lift the tray out of the trough you will find rubies and diamonds that can be made into rings, bracelets... whatever. Right. It is a nasty experience as far as I am concerned, but my kids always come away happy with the nuggets of great value they have found.

In the same way, we need to sift through the defeats of our past for a nugget of truth. Every painful experience contains one. I can now look back at the time I spent in the pit of depression and see so many diamonds. From the fiery coals of trails and struggles come jewels—treasures and truths that can only be realized through pain. One of the purposes of the darkness is to purify.

God did not come to eliminate the darkness. He did not come to explain the darkness. God came to fill the darkness with His presence.

In Isaiah 45:3, God promises, "I will give you the treasure of darkness, riches stored in secret places, so that you may know that I am the LORD, the God of Israel, who summons you by name." This verse promises that He has gone before us and in every trial, in every dark circumstance, buried a treasure or stored a rich secret that we can only find if we go through that trial and experience that darkness. Every defeat contains a treasure.

We must strain every defeat through Romans 8:28, which tells us that "in all things God works for the good of those who love him, who have been called according to his purpose." If this promise is true, then we need to confront the defeats of our past, disarm them, and compel them to surrender a seed of victory. Now a tiny seed may not seem like much, but never underestimate its power.

When Danna was in kindergarten, she came home one day with a paper towel tightly wadded up in her little hand. When I asked her what she had, she carefully unfolded the towel to reveal the biggest mess of mismatched and broken seeds I had ever seen. "Danna, what are you going to do with those seeds?" I asked. She looked up at me with her huge brown eyes and said she was going to plant them. I thought for a moment and said, "Honey, if those seeds don't grow, we will buy some brand new seeds to plant." I could see by the look on her face that she was offended by my lack of faith and replied, "They will grow, Mama. I prayed about it." She then grabbed a small paper cup from the kitchen pantry and marched outside to the flower bed in the front yard, where absolutely nothing will grow because the soil is so rocky. She filled the cup with dirt and with great determination, stuffed the seeds deep into the soil.

At this point, I had to say something. God's reputation was on the line. "Danna, let's run to the store and get some new seeds," I offered. She did not look at me as she walked back into the house, placed the cup under the kitchen faucet, and turned it on full blast. Seeds and dirt went everywhere. "Lord, are You paying attention?" I asked. Without even a glance in my direction, she marched out to the back porch and placed the cup on the windowsill, which is completely shaded at all times. "They need sunshine to grow," she said, her flashing eyes daring me to speak. She headed for her room with the parting challenge "You'll see." I began to prepare words of comfort for the disappointment that was sure to come.

Do you know what happened to those seeds? In three days, the cup was overflowing with green sprouts. Never underestimate the power of one tiny seed—nor the faith of one determined five-year-old.

We may need to take action in order to find that seed of victory. It may mean that we need to confess a sin or mend a broken relationship. Maybe there is someone we need to ask for forgiveness, or we may first need to forgive ourselves. When we take that action of obedience, the seed will be ours, and even the smallest seed can produce great victory.

David knew this truth. He had a lot of defeats, but he faced them, confessed them, and discovered seeds of restoration. Another chance. A new beginning. Remember that every trial, every defeat, every bit of darkness is wrapped around a powerful seed.

## THIRD TRUTH: ACCEPT THE CONSEQUENCES

The choices we make have eternal results. Our actions have consequences, and we must learn to accept those consequences. Galatians 6:7 gives us a warning: "Do not be deceived: God cannot be mocked. A man reaps what he sows." We keep planting lemons while expecting apples to grow. There are consequences to our actions, but we have become experts at creating ways to avoid them. We try to shift the blame. We rationalize and compare ourselves to others who have made greater mistakes. We even try to rewrite the rules so that they accommodate our sin. Numbers 32:23 says that we can be sure that our sin will "catch up" with us (TLB). Why would a loving God say this? Why must there be consequences to our sin when we are forgiven?

The first reason is that it's the law. Sin is always accompanied by painful consequences because consequences are a great deterrent to sin. David lost a child, his throne, and his health because of his sin.

The second reason is that our Father is absolutely committed to forming in us the character of His son. In other words, God is out to make us like Jesus Christ. Those consequences are expressions of God's love. Hebrews 12:11 explains it this way: "No discipline seems pleasant at the time, but painful. Later on, however, it produces a harvest of righteousness and peace for those who have been trained by it." When we are experiencing the consequences of our actions, we are being trained in righteousness.

> *Truth does not change. We must change in response to the truth.*

You may have heard of Carol Everett, the woman who opened the first abortion clinic in Dallas, Texas. She was very wealthy and very successful. Then she encountered Christ and knew her life had to change. She walked away from the money and the success, giving her life totally to Him. The following months were filled with great joy as well as incredible pain because the life that she had worked so hard to build began to crumble around her feet. Carol made the difficult financial decision to sell her home and called a Realtor named Norma Southerland, my mother-in-law. Mom is a great Realtor because she truly cares about her clients and is willing to get involved in their lives.

Carol became her client and her friend. Mom watched as Carol struggled to build a new life and walked through some very hard times. During this time, Mom and I were talking about the pain

Carol was experiencing. She didn't understand why Carol had to suffer when she had come to Christ and had been totally forgiven. It struck me that this was an example of having to accept the consequences of our actions. In reality, Carol was partly responsible for the death of many babies. Those consequences cannot be undone. But today, Carol travels extensively, sharing her story of God's unconditional love and forgiveness. God has blessed her life and changed countless others because of her willingness to accept the consequences. We must do the same.

## FOURTH TRUTH: LEARN THE LESSONS

There is only one thing more painful than learning from experience—and that is not learning from experience. Jesus is very clear in John 14:23-24 when He simply says, "If anyone loves me, he will obey my teaching...He who does not love me will not obey my teaching." Truth does not change. We must change in response to the truth. A learned truth is an applied truth. When we fail to learn from our mistakes, we are doomed to make those same mistakes again. It is like climbing the same old mountain over and over and over.

Every year, we take about one hundred people from our church to Ridgecrest, a training center in Asheville, North Carolina. There are classes in the morning and worship services every evening. But the afternoons are for playing. One of the favorite activities is tubing. The first year I went, we loaded up several vans and headed for the point in the river where we would begin. The road snaked through the mountains and lush countryside with few signs or markers. It soon became apparent we were lost. After several stops and a few wrong turns, we finally found the spot. We tumbled out of the vans, grabbed our inner tubes, and headed for the river, forgetting about the frustrating trip we had just endured. After a very refreshing afternoon in the icy waters of the Broad

River, we went back to the vans to head home. Someone suggested that we write the directions down. Good idea. But that's all it was…an idea. When we were lost again the next year, someone finally put the directions down on paper. The third year we got lost because the person that wrote them down forgot to bring them. We just kept going around the same old mountain, making the same wrong turns.

We can learn some very valuable lessons from the mistakes of our past. To avoid making the same mistakes over and over, we must go back and destroy the paths that led us in those wrong directions. Some of those paths may be old behavior patterns, certain friendships, or destructive habits. If a path leads to sin, if it makes it easier to sin, if it entices us to sin—we must run. We don't want to go down that road of devastation again. We've been there once before, and we know better.

David cried out to God. Then he made things right with everyone involved. In other words, he learned his lesson.

## FIFTH TRUTH: FORGIVE THE HURTS

Holding onto the hurts of yesterday is like playing with matches. You will get burned. Forgiveness is a vital part of dealing with the past. We must understand that forgiveness is a free gift. We cannot earn it nor will we ever be good enough to deserve it. But we must have it in order to get past our past.

We cannot forgive until we have first been forgiven. Psalm 103:10-12 is a lovely reminder of God's precious forgiveness. "He does not treat us as our sins deserve or repay us according to our iniquities. For as high as the heavens are above the earth, so great is his love for those who fear him; as far as the east is from the west, so far has he removed our transgressions from us." When we recognize that we are forgiven, we can then begin to forgive.

We must forgive ourselves before we can forgive others. If we refuse to forgive ourselves, we are saying that God's payment for our sin is not enough. But the Bible assures us that "if we confess our sins to Him [God], He is faithful and just to forgive us and to cleanse us from every wrong" (1 John 1:9 NLT). If God forgives us, then we must forgive ourselves.

Forgiving those who have hurt us is probably one of the greatest hindrances to getting past our past and one of the biggest reasons that we fall into the pit of depression. The hurts collect in our lives like stagnant water, creating darkness and death. There will be no freedom from the past until we release the pain and forgive. Colossians 3:13 instructs us to "make allowance for each other's faults and forgive the person who offends you. Remember, the Lord forgave you, so you must forgive others." This passage is very clear. We can stop forgiving others when God stops forgiving us.

As we are forgiven and as we forgive, we will find healing. Wounds become scars. Scars are signs of healing. Forgiveness is the thread of spiritual surgery. After David experienced forgiveness, he also experienced restoration. We must recognize that we are forgiven. We must forgive ourselves and others if we want to get past our past. We will talk more about forgiveness in the next chapter.

## Sixth Truth: Let Go and Walk On

It is true that we must deal with our past, but you can't go back and just "fix" it. There is a time to forget what you were and focus on what you can be. There is a time to let go and walk on.

The natives of Africa have an ingenious plan for catching monkeys. They hollow out coconut shells and fill them with cocoa beans. Monkeys love cocoa beans. The natives tie the shells to the trunk of a tree and leave it for the night. In the morning, they come back and round up all the monkeys. You see, a monkey will come along, smell the cocoa beans, and reach inside one of the shells to grab the delicious treat. It wraps its fingers around the beans and tries to remove its fist. But because the hole is much smaller than its fist, the monkey is unable to pull out its fist without releasing the beans. The monkey is trapped. It can escape if it will release what it is holding on to—but it refuses to let go.

What are you holding on to from your past that is holding you prisoner, robbing you of joy today? David let go of his past and came back to his Father. He remembered the victories, confronted his defeats, accepted the consequences, learned the lessons, and forgave the hurts. And God said, "He is a man after my own heart." Wow! If David can get past his past, so can we.

# 4

# Discovering *the* Power *of* Forgiveness

A STORY IS TOLD IN SPAIN of a father and his teenage son whose relationship had become strained. The list of hurts eventually grew so long and so deep that the son ran away from home. The father began to search for him.

After months of failure the father made one last desperate effort. He put an ad in a major newspaper of Madrid hoping to catch the attention of his son. "Dear Paco, meet me in front of the newspaper office at noon. All is forgiven. I love you. Your father." The next day at noon, in front of the newspaper office, 800 Pacos showed up, each one seeking forgiveness from his father.

We all need forgiveness. We all must learn how to forgive. Forgiveness is a powerful weapon of defense against the enemies of darkness and depression. Yet many times, we collect hurts, storing them in the secluded corners of our lives, thinking that hiding them robs them of their power. One of depression's favorite places to grow is in an unforgiving heart as it feeds on those hidden hurts and private pains.

As I sat in the darkness, I began to realize my heart was filled with a raging anger. Before my eyes marched a parade of agony that had lain carefully buried and unresolved in my heart since childhood. With each new wound it became increasingly harder to keep that fierce anger contained until it finally spilled out into my life, washing me over the edge of light and into the dark pit where I now sat. I realized I would have to face every one of those awful memories…feel each pain…relive every hurt…deal with it…and bury it in the sea of forgiveness.

How do we learn to practice true forgiveness? Jesus answers this question with a parable, an earthly story with a heavenly meaning.

> Then Peter came to Jesus and asked, "Lord, how many times shall I forgive my brother when he sins against me? Up to seven times?" Jesus answered, "I tell you, not seven times, but seventy-seven times. Therefore, the kingdom of heaven is like a king who wanted to settle accounts with his servants. As he began the settlement, a man who owed him ten thousand talents was brought to him. Since he was not able to pay, the master ordered that he and his wife and his children and all that he had be sold to repay the debt. The servant fell on his knees before him. 'Be patient with me,' he begged, 'and I will pay back everything.' The servant's master took pity on him, canceled the debt and let him go. But when that servant went out, he found one of his fellow servants who owed him a hundred denarii. He grabbed him and began to choke him. 'Pay back what you owe me,' he demanded. His fellow servant fell to his knees and begged him, 'Be patient with me, and I will pay you back.' But he refused. Instead, he went off and had the man thrown into prison until he could pay the debt. When the other servants saw what had

happened, they were greatly distressed and went and told their master everything that had happened. Then the master called the servant in. 'You wicked servant,' he said, 'I canceled all that debt of yours because you begged me to. Shouldn't you have had mercy on your fellow servant just as I had on you?' In anger his master turned him over to the jailers to be tortured, until he should pay back all he owed. This is how my heavenly Father will treat each of you unless you forgive your brother from your heart" (Matthew 18:21-35).

In this parable we find five steps that will enable us to experience the power of forgiveness and guard our hearts against depression.

> *We cannot really forgive until we have really been forgiven.*

## Step One: Experience True Forgiveness

"The servant's master took pity on him" (Matthew 18:27). The master was a man of great compassion and empathy. I believe the reason he took pity on the servant was because he had experienced forgiveness in his own life and learned the power of shared sorrow. He was a king. He was successful. Success is always built upon failure. Success is always accompanied by mistakes and often involves hurt and rejection. This king had certainly made mistakes and seen his share of failure. I am sure he had also been wronged. But he obviously had been forgiven and had learned how to forgive, because instead of responding to the servant in anger, he responded in compassion.

We cannot really forgive until we have really been forgiven.

"Be kind and loving to each other. Forgive each other just as God forgave you in Christ" (Ephesians 4:32 NCV).

Forgiveness was born on a cross, where a perfect Man died for imperfect people. There, at Calvary, Jesus laid down His pain and hurt, and through absolute rejection loved and forgave. Out of that forgiveness, He freed us to forgive ourselves as well as others. In Ephesians 1:7 we find life-changing news: "In Christ we are set free by the blood of His death. And so we have forgiveness of sins because of God's rich grace" (NCV). The greatest need of our lives is forgiveness. God provided for that need. "For God so loved the world that he gave his only Son, so that everyone who believes in him will not perish but have eternal life" (John 3:16 NLT).

A little boy went to see the Washington Monument in Washington, D.C. When he arrived, he pointed up at the monument and announced to the guard on duty, "I want to buy it." The guard asked, "How much do you have?"

The boy reached into his pocket and pulled out a quarter. The guard said, "That is not enough." The little boy replied, "I thought that you would say that," and pulled out nine more cents. The guard looked down at the small boy and said, "You need to understand three things. First, thirty-four cents is not enough. Second, the Washington Monument has never been nor will it ever be for sale. Third, if you are an American citizen, then the Washington Monument already belongs to you."

We need to understand three things about forgiveness. First, we can never be good enough or do enough to purchase it. Second, forgiveness is not for sale nor can we earn it. Third, if we have a personal relationship with Jesus Christ, then all of the forgiveness we will ever need already belongs to us. But we must choose to experience that forgiveness by accepting it as a free gift of God. To discover the power of forgiveness, we must first experience true forgiveness in our lives.

## STEP TWO: BE WILLING TO TAKE THE INITIATIVE

The story is told of a brother and sister who had a heated argument. Their parents told them they needed to make things right and forgive each other, but neither one would budge. They went to bed early, still seething with anger. At 2:00 A.M. a violent thunderstorm ripped through their neighborhood. When the mother went to check on them, they were not in their beds. Through the darkness she called, "Where are you?" A small, frightened voice answered, "We are in the closet forgiving each other."

A crisis or storm can cause us to move toward resolving conflict and choosing to forgive. Many times we refuse to forgive because of pride. We have been hurt. We have been wronged. Our rights have been violated. We wait for the other person to take the first step.

Notice how Peter asks the Lord his question about forgiveness. "Lord, how many times shall I forgive my brother when he sins against me?" (Matthew 18:24). What arrogance. Peter was much more concerned about the wrong done to him than about doing wrong to someone else.

The king in Jesus' story had every reason not to forgive the servant. The tax in Palestine was about eight hundred talents a year. The servant owed a whopping ten thousand talents. In today's economy, that is a lot of money! However, "the servant's master took pity on him, canceled the debt and let him go" (Matthew 18:27).

> *God is very serious about forgiveness.*

We need to be like that king, willing to take the first step in the process of forgiveness. Jesus was. Romans 5:8 tells us that "God shows his great love for us in this way: Christ died for us while we were still sinners" (NCV). He did not wait until we shaped up. He did not wait until we cleaned up our act. He did not even wait until we asked for forgiveness or knew we needed to be forgiven. Jesus stepped out of heaven onto a cross, purchasing true forgiveness for us. He died for people just like this servant: people who do not deserve forgiveness, people who refuse to ask for forgiveness, people who ignore their own faults, people who sit in judgment of others, people who insist on others taking the first step. The king understood the importance of keeping his forgiveness accounts settled. He understood the power that living in "forgiveness gear" brings to our lives.

"If you are standing before the altar in the Temple, offering a sacrifice to God, and you suddenly remember that someone has something against you, leave your sacrifice there beside the altar. Go and be reconciled to that person. Then come and offer your sacrifice to God" (Matthew 5:23 NLT). God is very serious about forgiveness. He wants us to understand that it doesn't matter how much we do. If we have not forgiven someone, if we know that someone has not forgiven us, we should drop everything, put life on hold, and make things right. In this verse, God implies that our service is unacceptable and that all of our very best gifts and efforts are absolutely worthless if they come from an unforgiving heart.

If we want to experience the power of forgiveness, we must be willing to nail our pride to the cross and take the initiative.

## STEP THREE: CANCEL THE DEBT

When we forgive, we choose to cancel the debt, sending it away as if it never existed. Forgiveness is a choice that leads to a deliberate action and then to an attitude. The servant did not ask for forgiveness because he was sorry for the debt. He was just sorry he got caught in the debt. He did not deserve forgiveness.

None of us do. He had no intention of repaying the king, and the king knew it. In the economy of that day, the servant would have had to work 20 years just to earn what he owed. In other words, his case was hopeless…except for one thing. The king was a man of compassion…a man who had experienced the power of forgiveness. The king assumed the loss. He chose to forgive and to cancel the debt.

I love the story of the little girl who was sitting on Santa's lap, giving him her list of very expensive toys she wanted for Christmas. When her list was completed, without one word of appreciation, she jumped off Santa's lap and ran toward her embarrassed mother standing in the crowd. "Honey, haven't you forgotten something?" the mother asked. The little girl thought for a moment and then said, "Oh, yes." Turning back to Santa, she shouted, "Charge it!"

God has already "charged" our sins to His Son's account, which paid the price for our forgiveness in full. He has canceled our eternal debt. To experience the power of forgiveness in our lives, we must choose to cancel the debts of those who have hurt us…forgiving as we have been forgiven.

> When you were spiritually dead because of your sins and because you were not free from the power of your sinful self, God made you alive with Christ, and He forgave all our sins. He canceled the debt, which listed all the rules we failed to follow. He took away that record with its rules and nailed it to the cross (Colossians 2:13-14 NCV).

## STEP FOUR: LET GO OF THE HURT

This king not only forgave the debt, but he let the debtor go free, just the way Jesus does. That is true forgiveness.

Micah 7:18-19 describes the forgiveness of God:

There is no God like you. You forgive those who are guilty of sin; you don't look at the sins of your people who are left alive. You will not stay angry forever, because you enjoy being kind. You will have mercy on us again; you will conquer our sins. You will throw away all our sins into the deepest part of the sea (NCV).

A little boy and his mom had gone shopping at the mall. The little boy had acted very badly, whining, wanting everything he saw, and running away from his mother.

As they were driving home he could tell his mom was very angry. He looked over at her and said, "When we are bad and we ask God to forgive us, He does, doesn't He?" His mom glanced at him and replied, "Yes, He does." "And when He forgives us He buries our sins in the deepest sea, doesn't he?" The mom answered, "Yes, that is what the Bible teaches." The little boy sat in silence for a while, and then he said, "I've asked God to forgive me. But I bet when we get home, you're going to go fishing for those sins, aren't you?"

Part of true forgiveness is releasing the hurt, letting go of the pain. When we don't, it becomes a constant spiritual and emotional drain, robbing us of joy, peace…even light. To experience the power of forgiveness, we have to quit fishing in the emotional waters of our past.

I love superglue and use it for everything. Not too long ago I was trying to repair a miniature tea set that our dog, Scruffy, had broken. I got out my trusty superglue and went to work. I glued the broken saucer and held it in place for 30 seconds, only to discover that I had glued my finger to the saucer. After several painful minutes of struggling to work my finger loose, I was free. The experience reminded me of forgiveness. When we refuse to release people from the hurt they have caused us, we are gluing them to their mistakes. When we cling to pain they have caused us, we are refusing to see them as more than something that they have done.

Psalm 103:12 reminds us that "He has removed our rebellious acts as far away from us as the east is from the west"(NLT). When we accept the forgiveness of God, He separates us from our sins. Then He calls us to do the same with the people in our lives. Nowhere does God say that we have to feel like forgiving. He just commands us to forgive. Our feelings are irrelevant. Our obedience is what matters.

Forgiveness is an independent act between God and us. It is totally separate from the response or reaction of the person we are forgiving. We are not responsible for their reaction; that responsibility belongs to them and to God. Our responsibility is to forgive. When we refuse to forgive, we not only harm ourselves, we become a hindrance to God working in their lives. "Now it is time to forgive him and comfort him. Otherwise he may become so discouraged that he won't be able to recover" (2 Corinthians 2:7 NLT).

Anytime that we impede the work of God we are in a dangerous position. It is time to let go of the hurt. It is time to forgive.

## STEP FIVE: MAKE FORGIVENESS A HABIT

I imagine Peter felt pretty good about his generous willingness to forgive "up to seven times" (Matthew 18:21). The traditional teaching of the rabbis was that an offended person needed to forgive a brother only three times. The answer of Jesus must have come as a shock.

Seventy times seven? Four hundred and ninety times. How could anyone even keep a record of that many wrongs? Exactly. That was the point that Jesus was trying to make. We are not supposed to keep a record of the wrongs done to us. "[Love] keeps no record of wrongs" (1 Corinthians 13:5).

There should be no limit to our forgiveness because there is no limit to His. Forgiveness should be given in the same measure that it is received. The first servant had been forgiven everything. He should have been willing to forgive in the same way. But because he refused to forgive as he had been forgiven, he was thrown into jail. When we refuse to forgive, we find ourselves behind emotional bars, trapped in a deep, dark pit of suppressed anger and painful chaos. An unforgiving heart will always turn into a bitter heart, making us a prisoner of our own bitterness. Then the person we are unwilling to forgive becomes our jailer. Like the king, we must live in "forgiveness gear"—committed to being right with each other—waging peace in every relationship.

John 13:35 reminds us of the importance of right relationships. "Your love for one another will prove to the world that you are my disciples" (NLT). Our relationships should be living illustrations of the love and forgiveness of God. We are never more like God than when we are practicing forgiveness.

I grew up in a small town in Texas. Our family doctor was our friend. I babysat for him. My mother was a nurse and worked with him. He took care of our medical needs, many times charging us nothing for his services. He was my friend, a man I respected, and a man I trusted—until the day he molested me.

In dealing with this hurt I considered several choices. Murder crossed my mind. Torture seemed reasonable. Dismemberment was a real consideration. But none of those seemed quite right.

I could choose to hang on to my anger and bitterness, making him my jailer, surrendering to him a measure of power and control, or I could choose to forgive him and set myself free. But I just couldn't forgive him by myself. So I asked God to help me. And He taught me a life-changing truth.

Colossians 3:13 says it this way: "If someone does wrong to you, forgive that person because the Lord forgave you" (NCV).

If we make the choice to forgive, God will supply the forgiveness.

We must make forgiveness a habit in our lives.

# 5

# Experiencing *the* Power *of* Right Thinking

WILL ROGERS ONCE SAID, "What the country needs is dirtier fingernails and cleaner minds." How true! Yet one of the dangers of depression is that it breeds wrong thinking. Irrational thought patterns, anxious imaginings, and contemplation of destruction and death grow abundantly in the pit. In the light, these thoughts seem absurd and harmless, but the cloak of darkness hides their danger. The reality is that if we think wrong, we will live wrong. The opposite is also true. If we want to live right, we must think right. Right thinking produces right living.

There is a famous scene in *Peter Pan*. Peter is in the children's bedroom. They have seen him fly and they want to fly too. They have tried it from the floor. They have tried it from the beds. The result is failure. Finally, John asks, "How do you do it?" Peter answers: "You just think lovely, wonderful thoughts and they lift you up in the air."

In a sense, the same is true for the believer. We can change our lives by changing the way we think. As I sat in the pit of depression, I began to see how destructive and self-centered my thought patterns had become. I also began to realize that this was the greatest source of apprehension and anxiety in my life. My thoughts had become a vicious cycle of self-condemnation and insecurity. Somehow the cycle had to be broken. I began to pray for direction, asking God to take control, knowing that only He could accomplish what I was asking. The steps that follow have literally reprogrammed my thinking processes and transformed my life.

## STEP ONE: RECOGNIZE THE POWER OF YOUR THOUGHTS

The greatest battlefield for the Christian is the mind. The mind is a garden that can be cultivated to produce the harvest we desire. The mind is a workshop where the important decisions of life and eternity are made. The mind is an armory where we forge the weapons for our victory or our destruction. The mind is a place where all the decisive battles of life are won or lost.

Proverbs 23:7 says it this way: "For as he thinks within himself, so he is" (NASB). In other words, what we think about we will become. My husband, Dan, was a youth pastor for many years. One night he was teaching on this subject. A young man in the back of the room raised his hand. He had a very concerned look on his face as he asked, "Dan, does this mean I am going to become a girl?"

Our thoughts are real and powerful—but that is not exactly what this verse means. It means that what we think about influences what we become. Our actions, our attitudes, our habits are born in the mind—in our thought lives. It stands to reason, therefore, that we can change our lives by changing what we think about. Isaiah 26:3 gives us the promise: "You will keep in perfect peace all who trust in you, whose thoughts are fixed on you!" (NLT). Peace and joy involve both the heart and the mind. Wrong thinking will lead to wrong living. The first step toward a right thought life is to recognize the power of our thoughts.

## STEP TWO: KNOW GOD'S STANDARD FOR YOUR THOUGHT LIFE

I call Philippians 4:8 God's trash can for the mind. "Finally, brothers, whatever is true, whatever is noble, whatever is right, whatever is pure, whatever is lovely, whatever is admirable—if anything is excellent or praiseworthy—think about such things." It is a purification system for our thought lives, a tool we can use to examine every thought and determine if it is worthy to dwell in the mind of God's child. In this verse God gives us five standards for our thought lives.

> *We must harness our thoughts and make them dwell on truth.*

*First Standard: True Thoughts ("whatever is true...")*

True thoughts are genuine, authentic, and sincere. According to Webster's dictionary, the word "sincere" comes from two Latin words meaning "without wax."

During Jesus' day, the artists of Middle Eastern countries created very expensive statuettes from fine porcelain. These figurines were so fragile that they would often crack when fired in a kiln. Dishonest dealers would buy the cracked figurines at a much lower price. They would then fill the cracks with wax before selling them. The honest merchants would display only the figurines that had no cracks and would post signs that read *sine cera*—which meant "without wax."

We must train our minds to think sincere and true thoughts.

We must harness our thoughts and make them dwell on truth We choose what occupies our minds. If our minds are not filled with good, the enemy will fill them with bad. Satan is a liar, and he uses lies as his main weapon.

"[The Devil] was a murderer from the beginning and has always hated the truth. There is no truth in him. When he lies, it is consistent with his character; for he is a liar and the father of lies" (John 8:44 NLT).

The devil wants to control our minds through lies because when we believe truth, the Holy Spirit takes over. When we feed our thought lives a steady diet of truth, we are inviting the Holy Spirit to work. When we believe a lie, Satan steps in. He sticks his hairy toe (I have never seen it, but I just know it is ugly and hairy) in the wall of our minds and catapults into our lives, wreaking havoc and hellish destruction.

He will lie to you about:

- the way you look
- your relationships
- your worth
- your fears
- your dreams
- your identity
- your God

Orel Hershiser, a great major league pitcher who pitched many years for the Dodgers, describes an encounter with his manager, Tommy Lasorda, which changed his life. Lasorda called him into his office and shouted at Hershiser, "You don't believe in yourself. You're scared to pitch in the big leagues. Who do you think these hitters are, Babe Ruth? Ruth's dead. You've got good stuff. If you didn't, I wouldn't have hired you. I've seen guys come and go, son, and you've got it. Be aggressive. Be a bulldog out there. That's gonna be your new name: Bulldog. With that name, you'll scare the batters to death. Starting today I want you to believe that you are the best pitcher in baseball. Look at that hitter and say, 'There's no way you can ever hit me.'" Two days later Orel pitched, and in three innings he gave up only one run. Lasorda's talk had worked. He calls it his "sermon on the mound."

We must refuse lies and fill our minds with truth. The only source of absolute truth is God's Word. As we digest it, as we take it into our lives and saturate our thoughts with it, we will be able to discern between what is truth and what is a lie.

First Corinthians 2:16 reminds us that we have the mind of Christ. The moment we come to Christ in a personal relationship, He begins to renew our minds and substitute new ways of thinking for old ones. Our minds become conditioned to hunger and search for truth. When we find truth, the Holy Spirit enables us to understand it. How can we fill our minds with truth? It is very simple…by filling them with Scripture. Here is a simple plan for plugging the truth of God into our lives:

- choose a passage of Scripture
- write it down
- speak it out loud
- memorize it
- meditate on it
- share it

Here are a few of my favorite verses:

> We are troubled on every side, yet not distressed; we are perplexed, but not in despair; persecuted, but not

forsaken; cast down, but not destroyed (2 Corinthians 4:8-9 KJV).

The LORD is my light and my salvation; whom shall I fear? The LORD is the strength of my life; of whom shall I be afraid? (Psalm 27:1 NKJV).

Trust in the LORD with all your heart and lean not on your own understanding; in all your ways acknowledge him, and he will make your paths straight (Proverbs 3:5-6).

What life-changing power is found in the Word of God!

A tourist was traveling in Alaska during the building of the Alaskan pipeline. In his travels, he came across a road sign that read, "Be careful which rut you choose. You'll be in it for the next 200 miles."

We all know how to get stuck in the rut of worry. We allow negative thoughts to create a rut in our minds, giving them access to our lives. But when we fill our minds with Scripture, we fill in those old ruts with peace and create new ruts—new thought patterns, thought patterns that are right. Then we are thinking God's thoughts. And when we begin to think God's thoughts, our thoughts will become true.

## Second Standard: Honorable Thoughts ("whatever is noble... whatever is admirable...")

The word "noble" is used only a few times in the New Testament. Each time it is linked to self-control, specifically to control of the tongue, and urges us to speak words of honor and respect.

The word "admirable" is similar to noble and carries the idea that our thought life should be worth talking about. In other words, if we think right we will speak right. Statistics say that the average person spends one-fifth of his or her life talking. (For us ladies, it might be a slightly higher percentage.) If all of our words were put into print, the result would be this: A single day's words would fill a 50-page book; in a year's time the average person's words would fill 90 books of 200 pages each.

What kind of book did you write today? Was it honorable? Was it one of encouragement or condemnation, love or hatred, peace or anger? Proverbs 16:24 reminds us that "pleasant words are a honeycomb, sweet to the soul and healing to the bones." James had this to say about the way we talk: "For we all stumble in many ways. If anyone does not stumble in what he says, he is a perfect man, able to bridle the whole body as well" (James 3:2 NASB).

There is an ancient myth about a god of the sea known as Proteus, who had an unusual power. He could assume many different shapes and appearances. He could become a tree or a pebble, a lion or a dove, a serpent or a lamb and had little difficulty in changing from one form to another. Proteus reminds me of the human tongue. It can bless or curse. It can express praise or whisper slander. It can speak a word of encouragement or become an instrument of destruction. The control of the tongue begins in the mind. The bridle for our tongue is a controlled thought life… a thought life that is admirable…a thought life that is noble…a thought life that is fit for a child of the King. If our thoughts are honorable, our words will be honorable as well.

## *Third Standard: Right Thoughts ("whatever is right…")*

Right thoughts conform to God's standards and are the result of God's righteousness at work in our mind. Our world majors in gray standards, running from absolutes that are black and white, trying to rationalize away what is clearly innate truth. Right thinking is not gray or borderline. It does not ride a spiritual fence but conforms to God's standards. We must make a choice about who and what is going to control our thought lives. If we don't choose, we will become what James 1:8 describes as "a double-minded man, unstable in all he does." The New Living Translation says it this way: "They can't make up their minds. They waver back and forth in everything they do." E. Stanley Jones stated that "if you don't make up your mind, then your unmade mind will unmake you."

When an immigrant comes to America, before he can become a citizen he must renounce all his commitments and allegiance to his former homeland and pledge one hundred percent allegiance to America. Then and only then will the U.S. government grant him citizenship. Some of us have come to Christ. We are citizens of heaven. But our thought lives still reek of hell—our old homeland. We allow our minds to drift. We do not take charge of our thinking processes. We are undisciplined mentally.

Undisciplined thinking will always flow to our greatest weaknesses. The human mind will always set itself on something. We just have to decide what the setting will be. A mind filled with wrong thinking becomes fertile soil for temptations of all kinds.

A woman was married to a miser who never wanted her to spend any money. One day she told her husband she was going window-shopping. He said, "Look, but don't buy." A few hours later she came home with a new dress. "What is this?" her husband asked. She explained, "Well, I saw this dress and thought I'd just try it on for fun. When I did the devil said, 'It sure looks good on you.'" Her husband said, "Right, then you should have told him, 'Get thee behind me, Satan.'" "I did," she answered. "But when he got behind me, he said, 'Honey, it looks even better from the back.'"

We laugh about temptation. We have become flippant about sin. But we need to understand that the goal of the enemy is the total destruction of our lives. James 1:14-15 says, "Temptation comes from the lure of our own evil desires. These evil desires lead to evil actions, and evil actions lead to death" (NCV). Satan wants us to stay in the pit. Darkness is his specialty. He delights in peering over the edge of the hole, admiring his handiwork. The front line of the battle against him and against depression is the mind. Many times our thought lives are an open invitation to him. We need to renounce those old ways of thinking. We need to choose against wrong thinking and actively pursue thoughts that are right.

### Fourth Standard: Pure Thoughts ("whatever is pure...")

A pure thought is innocent and undefiled. Pure thinking is not tainted by moral impurity. It is a worship word, the picture of a sacrifice without blemish, fault, or weakness. In other words, our thought lives should be a sacrifice acceptable to God and fit to be brought into His presence.

> *The purity of our thoughts determines the purity of our lives.*

Have you ever watched an icicle as it is formed? A few years ago, we enjoyed a winter vacation in Vermont where a heavy snowstorm had arrived just ahead of us. Everything was covered in a soft blanket of white. Icicles hung like fragile crystal ornaments from tree limbs and rooftops. One lazy morning I sat curled up in front of a crackling fire, gazing out at the beautiful postcard scene before me.

I watched as the softly falling rain gradually turned to long strands of ice. The icicles formed one drop at a time until they were a foot long or more. An interesting process unfolded before me. If the water was clean, the icicle was clear and sparkled like a finely cut diamond in the sun. If the water was unclean, the icicle looked muddy and its beauty was spoiled.

Our lives are formed one thought at a time, one attitude at a time. The purity of our thoughts determines the purity of our lives. David, in Psalm 101:3, gives us this challenge: "I will refuse to look at anything vile and vulgar" (NLT). This standard needs to be the goal for our thought lives. To keep this commitment, to control our thoughts requires us to filter all outside influences and check out their content before we take them into our minds. We must choose to apply the standard of purity in:

- movies
- books
- television
- music
- relationships
- conversations

Our prayer should be like David's in Psalm 51:10: "Create in me a new, clean heart, O God, filled with clean thoughts and right desires" (TLB). A clean mind will produce right desires. Right desires will produce right habits. And right habits produce a life of power and joy, a life that is pleasing to God—a life that is right. The old adage is true: "Sow a thought, reap an action. Sow an action, reap a habit. Sow a habit, reap a character. Sow a character, reap a destiny." We need to think pure thoughts.

### Fifth Standard: Lovely Thoughts ("whatever is lovely...")

Lovely thoughts promote peace and love. The way we live is determined to a large degree by the "setting" of our minds. Minds set on unlovely thoughts such as revenge, anger, or criticism will produce lives that are magnets. These unlovely thoughts will attract more bitterness and resentment and give birth to conflict. How do we change this destructive pattern? By changing the setting of our minds.

Colossians 3:2 says, "Set your minds on things above, not on earthly things." This same verse in the New Living Translation is rendered "let heaven fill your thoughts." God is saying the mind of the Christian should be set on things above, the "higher" things in life, such as kindness, gentleness, and love. When this is the setting of our minds, God says we will become lovable. We will call forth love. We will promote peace. We will become more attractive—even beautiful.

According to one survey, every year in the United States we collectively buy each minute:

- 1484 tubes of lipstick (at a cost of $4566)
- 913 bottles of nail polish ($2055)
- 1324 containers of mascaras, eye shadows, and eyeliners ($6849)
- 2055 jars of skin care products ($12,785)

That's $1,575,300 an hour, all in the pursuit of beauty. And for some of us, it is still not enough. True beauty is from within and grows from a thought life that is lovely...a thought life that is right.

## STEP THREE: CHOOSE TO PRACTICE RIGHT THINKING

Let's look at Philippians 4:8-9 again: "If anything is excellent or praiseworthy—think about such things. Whatever you have learned or received or heard from me, or seen in me—put it into practice. And the God of peace will be with you."

Paul describes the standard for our thought lives as one of excellence, worth commending to others. In other words, our thought lives should be models and patterns others can follow. We should never waste the magnificent power of the mind on anything less. He is challenging us to raise the bar in our thinking, refusing to allow the "low things" of this world to inhabit our minds. We need to be relentless in directing our thoughts in the paths of excellence. We cannot separate our inner thoughts from our outward actions. We will live out our thought lives. We are indeed in a great battle. In order to win we must take our thought lives captive.

In 2 Corinthians 10:5 Paul writes, "We are taking every thought captive to the obedience of Christ" (NASB). The New Century Version gives even more power to this verse: "We capture every thought and make it give up and obey Christ."

The first and greatest commandment is to love the Lord your God with all your mind. (See Matthew 22:36-38.) Not a part of your mind, not most of your mind, but all of your mind. To love Him with your entire mind requires obedience to the standard God has given. Knowledge is never enough. God is not pleased with our knowledge of the truth if it doesn't result in the practice of that truth lived out in our daily lives.

He calls us to take action in response to His truth because action sets truth free in our lives to work and transform. We are told in James 1:22 that "it is a message to obey, not just to listen to. If you don't obey, you are only fooling yourself" (NLT). When we are confronted with the truth, we need to hear it, receive it, learn it, and then put it into practice. To know that our thoughts should be excellent and worthy of praise is not enough. We need to employ these standards as the referees of our thought lives.

My husband, Dan, coaches a soccer team on which both Jered and Danna play. Our team just finished a very successful soccer season. This is our third season in this particular sports club. Over the years, we have learned which referees are good. Some referees just show up for the game. They do not take charge until the game is out of control and I am forced to step in and help by offering my opinion of their calls. (My kids hate that.) However, there is one referee who is wonderful. When he walks onto the field, everyone knows exactly who is in charge. He is tough and calls everything. The kids sometimes complain about his firm handling of the game, but they are also glad to see him because he brings a security and peace to the field. Everyone knows his motto: "I don't allow any junk."

That is exactly what this standard will do for our thought lives— if we choose to practice it. It will make the right calls. It will toss out the "junk" and bring a security and peace to our lives. Several years ago, a submarine was being tested and had to remain submerged for many hours. When the ship returned to harbor, the captain was asked, "Do you have any damage from last night's storm?" The captain looked at him in surprise and said, "Storm? We didn't even know there was a storm." The sub had been so far down that it had reached the area of the ocean known to sailors as "the cushion of the sea." Huge waves and winds can whip the ocean, but these waters below are not even stirred. The thought life that pursues right standards will find a "cushion" from the storms of life. It is a hedge of protection and a source of unshakable peace.

A powerful deterrent of depression is a thought life fully surrendered to and controlled by God. How's your thought life? Using the checklist below, take a minute to evaluate your thoughts by the standard of Philippians 4:8.

Is it:

| | |
|---|---|
| __ true | __ noble |
| __ right | __ pure |
| __ lovely | __ admirable |
| __ excellent | __ praiseworthy |

Do you want power…peace…victory? Paul instructs us to "think on such things." My father-in-law collects antique irons. I have been with him at flea markets and garage sales as he carefully examines each iron before buying it. These irons are usually very rusty, sometimes covered in dirt, and extremely old. To be perfectly honest, they all look the same to me. One day I finally asked him, "Dad, how do you tell if an iron is any good?" His answer held great wisdom. "I have learned that the iron is only as good as its handle. If the handle is solid, then the iron is valuable."

The "handle" for our thought lives is made up of a willingness to recognize the power of our thoughts, a commitment to God's standard concerning the mind, and a choice to practice right thinking.

# 6

# Winning *over* Worry

THE PIT OF DEPRESSION is often swimming with worry. Many depressed people live constantly in worry mode. I worried about how I ended up in that pit. I worried about how I would or if I even could get out. I worried about how this struggle with depression would affect my family and our ministry. I worried about what people would think of me when they saw my weakness and failure. I worried about what had happened in the past and what the future might hold. In the darkness, worry made everything seem bigger and uglier than it really was. Worry had helped usher me into the pit, and worry was one of my prison's guards. I desperately wanted to trust God, exchanging my worry for His peace. I read countless books on worry and anxiety. I described in great detail my favorite worries to those who would listen. I memorized Scripture on anxiety and worry. I begged God to take the worry away. Instead, He did a great work in my heart and mind. He exposed the enemy of worry and prepared me to do battle with it.

Worry is wasted energy. Worry uses today's resources to try to fix tomorrow's problems. Worry is consuming and very unhealthy. I heard about a man who was hospitalized because of anxiety. He pressed his ear up against the wall of his hospital room, listening intently. A nurse came in to check on him. "Shhhhh," whispered the patient, and then he called the nurse over. She pressed her ear up against the wall and listened for a long time. "I can't hear a thing," she said finally. "I know," the man replied. "It's been like that all day."

It is amazing what we worry about. According to one survey, the ten worst human fears are:

1. speaking in front of a group
2. heights
3. insects and bugs
4. financial problems
5. deep water
6. sickness
7. death
8. flying
9. loneliness
10. dogs

Worry fits this world, but worry does not fit the picture of a joy-filled life, the life Jesus came to give us. Nothing will rob you of joy quicker than worry. God came so that we would not have to worry, and yet we continue to do so. There must be a way to win over worry. Once again, I would sit at His feet dumping each fear and worry into His capable hands, resting and waiting for deliverance. It came.

> Rejoice in the Lord always. I will say it again: Rejoice!
> Let your gentleness be evident to all. The Lord is near.

Do not be anxious about anything, but in everything, by prayer and petition, with thanksgiving, present your requests to God. And the peace of God, which transcends all understanding, will guard your hearts and your minds in Christ Jesus (Philippians 4:4-7).

> *Joy is a deeply rooted confidence that God is in control.*

In this passage God gives us the promise of peace. However, there are conditions to be met. There are actions we must take in order to experience peace and win over worry.

## ACTION ONE: CHOOSE JOY

"Rejoice in the Lord always I will say it again: Rejoice!" (Philippians 4:4). The Message says it this way: "Celebrate God all day, every day. I mean, *revel* in him!"

The author, Paul, is serious about joy. He tells us twice in this passage to rejoice. To rejoice is to practice the presence of God, taking delight in Him and choosing to be glad, no matter what the circumstances of life may be. Many times life makes it impossible to be happy. Happiness is not what Paul is calling us to.

Happiness is a cheap imitation of true joy. Joy is a deeply rooted confidence that God is in control.

Paul's situation when writing this letter was not exactly conducive for joy. He was in prison under Roman house arrest, awaiting trial and almost certain execution. Yet he tells us to rejoice. Don't miss this. What Paul is telling us is a life-changing truth. Our inner attitudes do not have to reflect our outward circumstances. In other words, we cannot always find joy in our circumstances, but we can always find joy in the Lord of the circumstances. "When anxiety was great within me, your consolation brought joy to my soul" (Psalm 94:19).

The tense of the verb "rejoice" translates "to keep on rejoicing." It is an ongoing command, a constant call to obedience. Obedience always begins with a choice and ultimately ends in joy. In John 15:10-11, Jesus links joy to obedience when He says, "If you obey my commands, you will remain in my love, just as I have obeyed my Father's commands and remain in his love. I have told you this so that my joy may be in you and that your joy may be complete." There is no way in this world to escape pain, but we can avoid joy.

The pursuit of joy is a matter of choice. Our first and most important choice is to come to the source of real joy...Jesus Christ. We must also choose to rejoice in the midst of every circumstance, good or bad. We must choose to focus on and accept His plan for our lives. We must choose a joyful perspective. A little boy asked his friend, "Wouldn't you hate to wear glasses all the time?" "No-o-o," the other boy answered slowly, "not if I had the kind Grandma wears. She sees how to fix a lot of things. She sees lots of nice things to do on rainy days—good things that other people call bad. And she always sees what you meant to do even if you mess things up. I asked her one day how she could see that way all the time, and she said it was the way she learned to look at things. So it must be her glasses."

We must choose to view life through glasses of joy. When we choose joy, we are choosing against worry.

## Action Two: Be Gentle

Philippians 4:5 gives an unusual directive concerning worry: "Let your gentleness be evident to all." The word "gentleness" literally means "humility, softness, and tenderness." We must be gentle with everyone. The Living Bible paraphrases "gentleness" as "unselfish and considerate." Any way you look at it, this truth is in direct opposition to the viewpoint of the world in which we live, where power and assertiveness gain respect while gentleness is viewed as weakness.

In God's eyes gentleness is a harnessed strength and a controlled power. What in the world does gentleness have to do with eliminating worry? How we treat people affects our peace. Many of us have lives filled with worry because we have relationships filled with conflict. When we are not gentle, conflict is the result. Worry and anxiety thrive in the atmosphere of conflict.

What does it mean to be gentle in our relationships?

## Gentleness Is Willing to Give Up Control

"The wisdom that comes from heaven is first of all pure and full of quiet gentleness...It allows discussion and is willing to yield to others" (James 3:17 TLB). Gentleness celebrates the differences in each other. I heard about a little girl who told her grandmother that she had three best friends and that they all went to different churches. The grandmother asked if that ever caused a problem. The little girl replied, "Oh, no. It doesn't matter if we go to different churches because we are all Republicans." Gentleness can always find a patch of common ground. It gives people room to grow and change. Gentleness doesn't control but is willing to yield or submit to one another in love.

## Gentleness Is Love in Action

"[Gentleness] is full of mercy and good deeds" (James 3:17 TLB). Gentleness does not sit idly by watching people suffer. Gentleness gets involved in people's lives. The first holiday season I endured during my depression was Thanksgiving. I was dreading it because no family was coming. My sneaky husband came up with a plan. He invited my sister and brother-in-law to come on a surprise visit from Texas. He picked them up at the airport, dropped them off at a local restaurant, and then picked me up. I will never forget walking into that restaurant to find my family there. Why did they come? Because Dan had called and said "she needs you." That was all it took. Gentleness is love in action.

### Gentleness Is Forgiving

"Therefore, as God's chosen people, holy and dearly loved, clothe yourselves with compassion, kindness, humility, gentleness and patience. Bear with each other and forgive whatever grievances you may have against one another. Forgive as the Lord forgave you" (Colossians 3:12-13). Gentleness is quick to give and receive forgiveness. Gentleness takes the responsibility to initiate forgiveness.

### Gentleness Wages Peace

"Pursue peace with all people" (Hebrews 12:14 NKJV). Gentleness does not retaliate but instead pursues peace. The goal of gentleness is unity. I've read that when a group of horses face attack from predators, they naturally use an extremely effective strategy. The horses stand in a circle, facing each other, and with their back legs kick out at the enemy. Donkeys do just the opposite. They face the enemy and kick each other.

When we are hurt, it is natural for us to want to hurt back. Let's face it—getting even is fun! But revenge was never meant for our hands. God says that it belongs to Him (Deuteronomy 32:35). I suspect the reason is that in our hands it is dangerous and destructive, but in His, it is a tool of restoration.

> *The most powerful weapon against worry is Scripture.*

When Jered was very small, he and his dad would work happily for hours in the garage building "important stuff." Jered loved all of his daddy's tools, especially the power tools, which Dan would not allow him to use. For Christmas we bought a small wooden workbench and several tools in a toolbox that Jered could call his own. He played with them for about ten minutes, decided they were "baby tools," and marched straight out to the garage in search of something with a little more "oomph." Dan quickly followed his determined son out the door with a plan in mind. Picking up an electric drill, he placed it in Jered's tiny hand. As expected, it tumbled to the ground. Dan explained the tool was too big for Jered's hands but just the right size for his. In Jered's hands, that drill would become a dangerous weapon, but in Daddy's hands, it was a constructive tool. Revenge is like that—destructive in the wrong hands but constructive in the right ones. The only right hands for revenge are the hands of a God committed to mercy and justice for everyone involved.

When we practice gentleness and pursue peace in our relationships, there will be less conflict, more unity, and fewer footholds for worry.

## ACTION THREE: BE AWARE OF HIS PRESENCE

Paul added some important words to his comments about rejoicing and gentleness: "The Lord is near" (Philippians 4:5).

Our prayer should not be "Lord, be with me." Our prayer should be "Lord, make me aware that You are with me." The more we are aware of God's presence, the less we will worry. How do we become aware of His presence?

### His Word

"For the word of God is living and active and sharper than any two-edged sword" (Hebrews 4:12 NASB). The most powerful weapon against worry is Scripture. Read it. Memorize it. Immerse your life in it. The Word of God grounds us. It gives us roots when the storms of life come. When worry comes, reject it. Deflect it with the sword of God's Word.

### Prayer

"Give all your worries to him, because he cares about you" (1 Peter 5:7 NCV). Prayer is simply conversation with God. Go to Him, giving Him your worries. Run to Him with your fears. That is your responsibility. His responsibility is to take care of you.

I read about a widow who had successfully raised a large family. She had six children of her own and adopted twelve others. She never seemed to worry. A reporter once asked her the secret of her peace and confidence. She said, "I'm not alone. I'm in a partnership. My partner is the Lord. Many years ago I said, 'Lord, I'll do the work and You do the worrying.' I have had peace ever since."

### Other Believers

"An enemy might defeat one person, but two people together can defend themselves; a rope that is woven of three strands is hard to break" (Ecclesiastes 4:12 NCV). When you share your fears with others they grow smaller because someone has shouldered the load with you. A shared load is a lighter load.

### Experience

"Every good thing given and every perfect gift is from above, coming down from the Father of lights, with whom there is no variation, or shifting shadow" (James 1:17 NASB). The more we know God, the more we will understand that He is who He says He is. The more we know Him, the more we will see that He is willing and able to work in our lives. We will naturally begin to trust Him and soon discover that He is faithful. There is not even a shadow of turning with Him.

So much of our worry is wrapped up in the unknown. The "known" victories of yesterday can destroy the fear of today's "unknown" because He is always the same. Hebrews 13:8 assures us that He is the same "yesterday and today and forever." Security comes when we realize we can truly count on Him. He allows the storms to come so we will learn to trust Him. God doesn't just allow storms. He monitors them. His presence empowers us to win over worry. When you are tempted to worry, go back over the books, remember the victories, and celebrate them again. The God who delivered you yesterday will deliver you today and tomorrow.

*Jehovah Shammah—"I am there." Jehovah Shalom—"I am your peace." Jehovah Jireh—"I am your provider." Emmanuel—"God with us."*

## ACTION FOUR: CHOOSE TO TRUST

Philippians 4:6 tells us something easy to comprehend but hard to put into practice: "Do not be anxious about anything."

The word "anxious" literally means "to be pulled in different directions." It is based on the old English root from which we get our word "worry" meaning "to strangle." Worry can strangle us, but trust breaks the stronghold of worry in our lives.

It is possible to not worry. It must be. God never asks us to do anything that He doesn't empower us to do. In Isaiah 41:10 He tells us, "Do not fear, for I am with you; do not be dismayed for

I am your God. I will strengthen you and help you; I will uphold you with my righteous right hand."

Worry is a control issue. Its opposite is trust. Choose to trust more, and you will worry less. Choose to worry more, and you will trust less. Choose to trust completely, and you will not worry. The choice is yours.

What a great promise we find in Isaiah 26:3: "You, LORD, give true peace to those who depend on you, because they trust you" (NCV). Why do they have peace? Because they trust God. Trust demands that we give Him first place in our lives.

Who is God in your life? Playing God is the root of worry. When we play God we are trusting in our own sufficiency. God commands us to give Him first place and live, as He wants us to, totally depending upon Him. Every opportunity to worry is also an opportunity to trust God. Choose trust.

When Danna was a toddler, she and her daddy had a game they loved to play. Dan would put her in some high place, hold out his arms, and say, "Jump to Daddy." Normally, Danna would bail off into her father's strong arms without hesitation. One day the jump seemed a little too high, and Danna was a little too frightened. She stood frozen to her spot and said, "I can't, Daddy. I can't see you." Dan immediately responded with the assurance "It's okay. I can see you." And she jumped into his arms!

Trust Him. He's there. He knows what He is doing. Even when you can't see Him, He can see you. And He is all sufficient. His arms are open and waiting for you.

## ACTION FIVE: PRAY ABOUT EVERYTHING

Paul follows "do not be anxious about anything" with "but in everything, by prayer and petition…present your requests to God" (Philippians 4:6).

The word "petition" means to earnestly plead with or to

implore. To "present your requests" is simply to "make known" or "tell" God specifically what it is that you need. We are encouraged in 1 Thessalonians 5:17 to "pray continually." The literal translation of "continually" is "in the direction of the sun." It is the idea of beginning first thing in the morning and not stopping. We are to pray about everything. Praying about everything shuts out worry because prayer invites God to be involved in every area of your life. When He is involved, we don't have to worry.

We have a portable phone, which I can never find because it is never in its holder. One day I was searching for this traveling phone and walked into the living room to find Danna on the couch with the phone in one hand and the remote control for the television in the other. "Are you talking to Amanda?" I asked. She responded, "Yes. We are watching TV together." I decided to come back later. When I did, the phone was on the sofa cushion beside her. I asked if I could please use the phone only to hear, "Mom, Amanda will be right back. She is eating dinner, but I want to keep the line open." That is the idea of praying without ceasing...the idea of keeping the line open.

I have heard it said that "when your knees knock, kneel on them." In other words, instead of worrying, pray.

## ACTION SIX: GIVE THANKS AND PRAISE HIM CONTINUALLY

Paul encourages the giving of thanks in our prayers: "but in everything...with thanksgiving" (Philippians 4:6). "Always give thanks to God the Father for everything in the name of our Lord Jesus Christ" (Ephesians 5:20 NCV)

When we lived in South Florida, the grass in our yard grew year round. We learned over the years that the best way to deal with weeds is to take care of the grass. When grass is healthy, weeds have no space to grow.

When our hearts and lives are filled with praise and thanksgiving, worry is a weed that will die from lack of attention. Why? Because praise acknowledges the very character of God, while thanksgiving recognizes the work of His hand. Together, praise and thanksgiving are powerful weapons against worry.

- Praise and thanksgiving pleases God. Psalm 147:1: "How good it is to sing praise to our God, how pleasant and fitting to praise him!"

- Praise and thanksgiving encourage obedience. First Thessalonians 5:16-18: "Be joyful always; pray continually; give thanks in all circumstances, for this is God's will for you in Christ Jesus." It is His will for us to praise Him. Obedience to Him always promotes peace and eliminates worry.

- Praise and thanksgiving enhance our awareness of His presence. Psalm 22:3: "But You are holy, enthroned in the praises of Israel" (NKJV). When we praise God we are enthroning Him in our lives. We are making that fearful circumstance His dwelling place.

- Praise and thanksgiving produce trust. Psalm 42:11 asks, "Why am I so sad? Why am I so upset? I should put my hope in God and keep praising Him, my Savior and my God" (NCV).

Thanksgiving is a deposit on the future. Praise is trusting Him for what He will do and then expecting Him to do it, understanding that today's stumbling blocks are tomorrow's stepping-stones. Praise frees God to work because when we praise Him we are trusting Him totally despite the circumstances.

The story is told of a young man who was sitting on a park bench reading his Bible. Suddenly he began to shout. "Praise the

Lord! What a miracle!" An older, very distinguished man walking by stopped and asked what he was so excited about. The young man replied, "I was just reading how God parted the Red Sea and the whole nation of Israel walked across on dry ground." The older man sneered, "Don't you know? That wasn't a real sea at all. It was just a few inches of water." He then turned in irritation and walked away, leaving the young man confused and discouraged. But in a few minutes he began to shout again. The unbeliever returned asking, "What are you shouting about now?" "Well, sir, I just read how God drowned the whole Egyptian army in just a few inches of water!"

Don't let anyone keep you from praising God. Don't let any circumstance deny you the joy of giving thanks. "I will thank the Lord at all times. My mouth will always praise Him" (Psalm 34:1 GWT). "Because of the LORD's great love we are not consumed, for his compassions never fail. They are new every morning; great is your faithfulness" (Lamentation 3:22-23).

If you want to win over worry, give thanks and praise to Him.

## A FINAL THOUGHT

Paul has shown us the actions we must take to win over worry:

- choose joy
- be gentle
- be aware of His presence
- choose to trust
- pray about everything
- give thanks and praise continually

Six conditions. Now here is the promise. "And the peace of God, which transcends all understanding, will guard your hearts and your minds in Christ Jesus" (Philippians 4:7). Peace ushers tranquility and a sense of calmness into the chaos of life. When peace reigns, we will be untroubled and have a sense of well-being.

Paul says that this kind of peace is beyond our understanding. It is beyond our ability to comprehend. The world cannot grasp it but would pay any price to have it.

This peace is not something that we can create on our own. It is a supernatural gift from God and is given to us as a hedge of protection. It will "guard your hearts and minds in Christ Jesus." In this verse, "guard" is a military term for "a garrison or stationed guard." When we have met the conditions, God stations peace at the doorway of our hearts and minds with the assignment, "Protect My child."

So the good news is that we can win over worry. What fear is gripping your heart? What are you worrying about? Give it up. Take action. Claim the promises and exchange your worries for God's gift of peace.

# 7

# Dealing *with* Stress

STRESS MANAGEMENT IS VITAL IF we want to avoid depression. When we do not know how to deal with the stress of everyday life, it drains and consumes us. Our inner resources are depleted, and we find ourselves at the bottom of the pit. I once saw a bumper sticker that read, "Just when I thought I was winning the rat race, along came faster rats." Stress is a familiar companion. It can destroy our health and damage every part of life. Stress has many clever disguises and can go unchecked until we find ourselves in trouble.

The years prior to my pit experience were laced with stress-related problems. I did not feel well physically and always seemed tired and irritable. A sense of impending doom would wake me in the middle of the night and hang over my days like a dark cloud. I began to have trouble sleeping, and migraines became almost a daily occurrence. Finally, severe stomach pain sent me running to the doctor, who ordered a battery of tests. For three months, the medical world searched for an answer. Every week there was a different awful test. Finally, the doctor looked at me and said,

"Mary, we can find absolutely nothing wrong with you except for one thing. Stress. Chronic stress is making you sick, and you must learn to deal with it."

I looked at him and said, "That's absurd. I tell people how to deal with stress. I am a pastor's wife. I am a Christian who is supposed to be living a life of joy and peace." The doctor did not seem to be very impressed. He handed me a list of stress-relievers and sent me on my way. I felt as though I had been offered a Band-Aid when I needed major surgery. I needed help, and fortunately I knew where to get it. I began to search the Scriptures for the answers and soon discovered that stress management is a spiritual discipline. There is no single secret to handling stress, but there are many keys in God's Word.

Sometimes the most well-known passages are the most overlooked. Psalm 23 is one of those passages. This psalm is the description of a personal relationship between sheep and shepherd, between child and father. It gives us ten keys for dealing with stress.

> The LORD is my shepherd; I shall not want. He makes me to lie down in green pastures; He leads me beside the still waters. He restores my soul; He leads me in the paths of righteousness for His name's sake. Yea, though I walk through the valley of the shadow of death, I will fear no evil; for You are with me; Your rod and Your staff, they comfort me. You prepare a table before me in the presence of my enemies; You anoint my head with oil; my cup runs over. Surely goodness and mercy shall follow me all the days of my life; and I will dwell in the house of the LORD forever (Psalm 23:1-6 NKJV).

## KEY ONE: KNOW WHOSE YOU ARE
(*"The Lord is my shepherd"*)

In handling stress we have to begin with a vital, personal relationship with a living Lord. It is very frustrating and quite stressful to try to live the Christian life when you are not a Christian. It is just as frustrating and maybe more stressful to be a Christian and have a broken relationship with Him.

I grew up going to church. I was there every time the doors were open. When I was ten years old, I joined the church. During a worship service, I walked down the aisle, shook the pastor's hand, and sat in the front row. The pastor asked me if I loved Jesus, and like any child, I said that I did. He pronounced me a Christian and had me fill out a church membership card. At the end of the service, everyone came by to hug me and welcome me into the "family." They were all crying and seemed very happy. They told me I had made the most important decision of my life. I didn't get it. All I had done was join the church. What was the big deal? I immediately plunged headlong into serving a God I did not know, trying desperately to make Him love me, trying to find whatever it was that was missing in my life.

The summer after my ninth grade year, our youth group went to Glorieta, New Mexico, for a youth conference. The preacher that week was Gregory Walcott, an actor whom I had seen in several Westerns. One night at the conclusion of his sermon, he looked out into the sea of young people, and pointed straight at me. His words pierced my heart. "If you died tonight," he asked, "where would you spend eternity?" And I knew. In that moment I knew what it was that was missing. I knew all about Jesus Christ, but I did not know Him. This truth washed over me and filled my heart with new understanding. He knew me, He loved me, and He was calling me. I looked up and panicked. I couldn't make a commitment to Christ in front of all those people. So I began bargaining with Christ, telling Him that as soon as I got home to my little church in Brownwood, Texas, I would get this whole thing settled.

Weeks passed as I stubbornly clutched my pride, refusing to give in to the One I needed the most. Finally, during a spring revival service at my church, the preacher was winding up his message. I hadn't paid attention to one word he had said until I heard the haunting question once again. "If you died tonight, do you know where you would spend eternity?" That night I made a life changing commitment, not to join a church, but to give myself to a living Lord.

That was a wonderful beginning, but there have been times in my life when my sin has marred that relationship. Sin that is not dealt with can make you doubt whose you are, but it can never change whose you are. If my son left home and never returned, he would still be my son. Our relationship would be strained, but nothing he does or doesn't do can change the fact that he is my son. Much of our stress comes from a faulty understanding of who we are and whose we are.

> *A loving Father meets the needs of His kids.*

Go back to the beginning. Examine your relationship with Jesus Christ. Do you know Him? Is your relationship right with Him? Is there sin that needs to be dealt with? Do you have a clean heart before Him? Do you know whose you are?

## KEY TWO: RECOGNIZE YOUR SOURCE *("I shall not want")*

A Sunday school teacher asked her class of first graders to quote their favorite verse. A little boy's hand shot up quickly. After the teacher called on him, he began reciting Psalm 23. "The Lord is my shepherd. He's all I want." The little boy may have quoted the verse wrong, but he got the central message right.

This verse is stating the fact that God will take care of us. The word "want" literally means "lack." In other words, as His child we will lack nothing. He will supply all of our needs. We sometimes confuse our needs and our greeds. We live in a world that honors the pursuit of things. It is hard not to get caught up in building a "Kingdom of Thingdom." Calvin Miller said, "The world is poor because her fortune is buried in the sky and all her treasure maps are of the earth."

A loving Father meets the needs of His kids. He is our source. Your spouse is not your source. Your job is not your source. Your children are not your source. So much of our stress comes from looking in the wrong places and to the wrong people for our needs to be met. Jesus Christ is our source.

## KEY THREE: KNOW WHEN TO BE STILL
*("He makes me lie down")*

Sleep is sacred. Sometimes the most spiritual thing you can do is sleep or get some much-needed rest. It is a medical fact that the human body is programmed for a certain amount of rest. We can cheat it short term, but not for long.

When we fail to get enough rest, the efficiency of the body is affected. We run on "batteries" that must be recharged on a regular basis. When we are tired, it is much harder to handle stress.

When Jered was eleven years old, he wanted a remote control car. We decided to get him one for Christmas. I bought it, installed batteries, wrapped it, and placed it under the tree. On Christmas morning, we made him open it last. When he tore into the present and realized what it was, he yelled for joy, gave us a hug, and headed outside with his sister to the driveway for a test run. Dan and I stole a few delicious minutes of quiet and then went to watch. What I saw did not make me happy. The car was running in short spurts and stammering circles. I couldn't believe it. That car had been expensive and was supposed to do all kinds of stunts, but in a matter of minutes it was broken. "Jered," I fumed, "what is the matter with this car? Is it already broken? Do we need to return it?" Jered calmly said, "It's okay, Mom. It just needs new batteries. I read the instructions, and they say that when the batteries are low the car will run in circles." When our batteries are low, we also run in circles.

If we look at our calendars, we might think fatigue is one of the spiritual gifts. This may come as a shock, but it isn't on the list. We not only need to learn how to rest; we must learn when to rest. We need to take the time to rest when we don't have the time to rest. When we can learn to "be still," our stress level will go down.

## Key Four: Learn the Value of Solitude
(*"still waters"*)

The analogy at the heart of Psalm 23 is that of God as the Shepherd and His children as the sheep. Sheep are never fully at ease around rushing water. They are very poor swimmers. They seem to sense that the weight of their wool, when wet, will drown them. Sheep need still water. They need quiet water. Psalm 46:10 tells us to "be still, and know that I am God." There is so much about God that is unknowable on the run. But this verse promises that when we are still, walking in quiet waters, we will know Him intimately. Stillness implies quietness and solitude. The more responsibility we carry, the busier we are, the more we need regular solitude.

Solitude does not just happen. We have to carve it out of our hectic days and make room for it. Life can become so crowded, leaving no room for the most important things, the eternal things.

We need time alone, sitting at the feet of Jesus, so that we might know Him. It is out of those quiet moments that His plan for our lives rises like the dawn. It is in solitude that we are replenished and restored to face the challenge of the day. We might think that we do not have time for solitude, but if we are wise, we will realize that solitude actually improves our time management. We must look for opportunities to practice solitude, and when they come, grab them.

Here are some tips for making the most of moments and hours just with yourself:

- Spend time outdoors. There is something so refreshing about spending time alone outside. Enjoy a day at the beach. Walk in the park. Sit in the shade of a tree and think. Lie down in the grass and watch the clouds drift by.
- Learn the art of "centering down." This is an old Quaker term referring to the practice of ordering your thoughts and centering them on God.
- Have days when you abandon all agendas.
- Be silent.
- Read God's Word and let it soak slowly into your spirit.
- Listen to quiet music.

How you practice solitude is not as important as the commitment to make solitude a regular part of your life.

## KEY FIVE: DO WHAT GOD GIVES YOU TO DO
*("He leads me in the paths of righteousness")*

The word "righteousness" means the "right things." The Shepherd has a plan for His sheep—and so does everyone else. The plan of the Shepherd is a perfect plan, a good plan. The Shepherd's plan will lead His sheep in the paths that are best for them. When the sheep choose to follow a different plan, they always wind up in trouble, lodged in some crevice or lost on the wrong path.

The Shepherd only empowers His agenda. First Thessalonians 5:24 promises, "Faithful is He who calls you, and He also will bring it to pass" (NASB). In other words, God empowers us to do what He calls us to do. When we step into our agenda, our plan, we are stepping into our own strength. We will soon be lost and running on empty.

The Father is not looking for perfection. He is looking for authenticity. Authenticity means that we must be who we are. We must become who God has gifted us to be. We don't please God when we try to be someone we are not. We can't glorify the Father with gifts we don't have. Find your gifts, the ones that He gave you, and use them. That is why He placed them in your life so that you could give them back to Him in service.

One way to discover these God-given gifts is to find your spiritual "shape." We all have a blueprint that was tucked into our being by the creative hand of a loving God. He loves watching us be us.

*...no valley is permanent.*

This acrostic from Pastor Rick Warren has helped many to discover their spiritual shape:

- S—spiritual gifts
- H—heart passion
- A—abilities and talents
- P—personality
- E—experiences of life*

As we discover what it is that God created us to do, we are set

* Used by permission.

free to eliminate everything in our lives that does not fit into that plan. Much of our stress comes when we try to be all things to all people. Do what God gives you to do and discover the joy of a purpose-driven life.

## KEY SIX: EXPECT SOME VALLEYS
*("Even though I walk through the valley of the shadow of death")*

Death comes to us in many ways and creates a suffocating stress that can be consuming. It might be the death of a loved one or a relationship. It could be the death of hope or a dream. But valleys will come.

We need an attitude adjustment for those valleys of life. Remember, no valley is permanent. My favorite four-word phrase in the Bible is "it came to pass." Every valley is surrounded by mountains and has a Shepherd. The Shepherd is familiar with the valley, because He has gone before the sheep and knows what lies ahead. He will walk through that valley with the sheep, out in front, leading the way. Any attack meant for the sheep must first go through Him. Expect some valleys, but know that He is the Shepherd of each one.

## KEY SEVEN: MANAGE YOUR FEARS
*("I will fear no evil; for You are with me")*

God's presence changes everything. My favorite two-word phrase in the Bible is "but God." I don't know what tomorrow holds, but God is with me. I am sick, but God is the Great Physician. I am lonely, but God promises to never leave or forsake me. I am afraid of the dark, but God is the Light of the world. When He comes, everything is different.

Verse 4 goes on to say, "Your rod and Your staff, they comfort me." The rod and staff are opposite ends of the same stick. The rod is the blunt end. The Shepherd uses it to fight off attackers. Sheep are defenseless creatures, so the Shepherd is totally responsible for their protection. The staff is the crooked end. The Shepherd uses it to pull the sheep out of tough places. Sheep are helpless, which means the Shepherd must constantly rescue them.

We have nothing to fear. We are His sheep. He will protect and defend us. He will reach into those dark places where we have fallen and lift us out. We can manage our fears by taking them to our Shepherd, the One who holds the rod and staff in His hand.

## KEY EIGHT: CELEBRATE THE BATTLE
*("You prepare a table before me in the presence of my enemies")*

The Hebrew people had the right idea. They had a victory banquet before the battle. There was an anointing on their lives, a sign of being chosen by God. They celebrated the battle's outcome because they knew they were chosen people. When the enemy comes, we need to sit down at the table of victory because God has chosen us to be His own and He is on our side. If God is for us, we win. Romans 8:31 declares, "If God is for us, who can be against us?" My husband often says, "If God is for us, who cares who is against us?"

The battle is for our good. Our greatest growth comes in the midst of our battles. My friend Kim lost her young son in a drowning accident. When we first met, she seemed like a fragile child trying to carry a heavy load of pain and suffering. But over the years I have seen her grow stronger with each step. She kept trusting and walking through her pain. Now she is a shining trophy of grace, quick to share her testimony of God's sufficiency in her darkest hour. He has used her to encourage others who have lost much. Kim would tell you that this horrible battle has been for her good. Only God can accomplish that.

Celebrate the battle, confident that He is with us. Celebrate the battle, recognizing that it is for our good. Celebrate the battle, knowing that we win.

## KEY NINE: COUNT ON GRACE
*("Surely goodness and mercy shall follow me all the days of my life")*

Because I can barely sew on buttons, I admire people who do needlepoint. I have a friend who does beautiful work. One day on our way to lunch, she showed me her latest project. I began to tell her how beautiful it was when she stopped me and told me to turn it over. When I looked at the back, I was surprised to see ugly knots, threads of all colors going every direction, and, in general, a big mess. From the front it was a beautiful work of art. From the back it was a total disaster.

Life is like that. It all depends on your perspective. You may be looking at the knots and messes of your life, wondering if anything good will ever come out of this disaster. But one day you will see it from the Father's perspective, a work of beauty.

God uses His mercy and loving kindness to create trophies of grace. Count on His grace.

## KEY TEN: TAKE THE LONG LOOK
*("I will dwell in the house of the LORD forever")*

I have said this before...Life is a marathon, not a 50-yard dash. It is a process, not a product. It is a journey, not a destination. We need to remember to live life, taking the long look. When Jered was a toddler, I took him to Sears for their picture special, the one that gives you about a hundred pictures for $3.99. I was surprised to find the studio empty for once. The photographer pulled down a blue backdrop to match my son's blue eyes and took the set of pictures included in the offer. When he had finished, no one else had come in and Jered was putting on quite a show. The photographer asked if I would mind if he took some extra shots for his studio. What mother would refuse an offer to have her son's picture plastered all over the walls of a photography studio? He handed me a black suit to put on Jered and pulled down a black backdrop. It was amazing to see how the different colors changed Jered's appearance. Each backdrop made him look just a little different.

We often think that our backdrop is made up of the circumstances of our lives. Don't be fooled. Our backdrop is eternity. Our backdrop is a cross. Our backdrop is an empty tomb. Take the long look. Remember who it is that will be your ultimate audience. Stress melts away when our glance is on the circumstance and our gaze is on Him.

## A Final Thought

Psalm 23 is one of the most-loved passages in the Bible for good reason. It offers phenomenal insight into how we should deal with stress. Let me challenge you to read Psalm 23 every day for one month. Plug it in to your life and let the truths of this rich passage enable you to manage stress.

# 8

# Managing Your Emotions

GOD MADE US EMOTIONAL CRITTERS. He created us with a great capacity for emotions so that our lives can be richer, fuller...seasoned. But like so many things created by His hand, our emotions have been misused, abused, and misunderstood until their correct place in our lives has been lost.

When we are emotionally bankrupt, we become an easy target for depression. The results are disastrous and far-reaching. Our lives are then plagued by physical disorders, emotional problems, wrecked relationships, destroyed ministries, and unfulfilled dreams.

Some would say we should just ignore our feelings, deny their existence, and stuff them down into a dark corner of the heart. I used that technique for most of my life. It doesn't work. Those suppressed feelings became an emotional cancer that silently but surely consumed my energy and created the perfect conditions for my journey into the pit of depression.

Stuffing emotions is not a biblical concept and negates much of God's Word. The most transparent man who ever walked the earth was Jesus Christ, the Son of God. His nature was to be open and honest, inviting others to tear down the emotional walls they had so carefully built. In the life of Jesus we see sorrow, anger, frustration, and even fear. The Bible records the emotional integrity of many others. Peter was afraid as he walked on the water to Jesus. Mary and Martha were devastated by the death of their brother, Lazarus. David was depressed because of the great sin in his life.

> *Correctly identifying emotions*
> *is essential to emotional healing.*

Some would say that the right way to manage emotions is simply to "let it all out" and give them free rein. Proverbs 25:28 describes the dangerous outcome of this approach: "Like a city whose walls are broken down is a man who lacks self-control." The New American Standard Bible says it this way: "Like a city that is broken into and without walls is a man who has no control over his spirit." Just as it is wrong to ignore or deny our emotions, it is just as wrong to give them freedom to roam through our lives, destroying everything and everyone in their path.

Emotions are not sin, but the place we give them in our lives and our response to them can be. So we have a choice to make. We can learn how to manage our emotions or decide to play it safe, letting them manage us.

One hot day in July, a farmer was sitting in front of his shack, smoking his corncob pipe. Along came a stranger who asked, "How's your cotton coming?" "Ain't got none," was the answer. "Didn't plant none. 'Fraid of the boll weevil." "Well, how's your corn?" "Didn't plant none. 'Fraid o' drought." "How about your potatoes?" "Ain't got none. Scairt o' tater bugs." The stranger finally asked, "Well, what did you plant?" "Nothin'," answered the farmer. "I just played it safe."

If we do not learn how to manage our emotions, we will spend our lives just playing it safe. Jesus Christ did not come so that we might have a safe life. He came so that we might have an abundant life. Our emotions are a gift from the hand of God and part of that rich abundance. With every gift from the hand of God comes the plan for using it in the right way. We can learn how to manage our emotions when we take the right steps.

## STEP ONE: IDENTIFY YOUR EMOTIONS

Before we can be honest and real about emotions, we must identify them. A correct medical diagnosis is essential to physical healing. Correctly identifying emotions is essential to emotional healing. Emotions have many masks and are masters of deception.

Some are positive. Some are negative. For the sake of this study, we will concentrate on those emotions that have a negative effect in our lives. These negative emotions seem to be the ones we struggle with the most in times of depression. How do we discover their true identity?

### Find the Source

Proverbs 23:7 tells us that "as he thinks within himself, so he is" (NASB). There are many sources of negative emotions. Daily life offers up a generous serving for us to digest. Past experiences can harbor negative emotions for a lifetime. Each time we experience hurt or rejection we are presented with the opportunity to accept negative emotions. Some people are "carriers." They walk through life, contagious with negative emotional baggage. Satan himself deals primarily in these destructive emotions and is always willing to share. Many times, the mind becomes a bed of negative emotions.

Pray, asking the Holy Spirit to reveal the sources of negative emotions in your life. That is one of His jobs. John 14:26 says, "The Holy Spirit, whom the Father will send in my name, will teach you everything, and remind you of all that I have said to you" (NRSV).

## Label Them Correctly

It is time to be honest about our emotions. It is time to stop denying that they exist. We must get real in order to get right. Healing and restoration begin at the point of emotional integrity. The revealing of your feeling is the beginning of your healing.

In chapter 1, I shared with you that when Dan and I first came to Flamingo Road, our church went through some radical changes in transitioning from a traditional model to a contemporary one. God called us to a unique ministry, one that was very different from the churches in which we had previously served. I loved the changes and felt certain God was leading us and directing us. I also hated the changes because they upset many of the people we called friends. Some left to join other churches that better fit their style of worship. Others left in a storm of criticism and hurt.

I had never experienced such pain and rejection. I knew I was not supposed to take it personally, but it was very personal. Instead of honestly dealing with the emotional damage, I plastered a spiritual smile on my face and pretended everything was fine. Everything was not fine. My joy was gone. There was a knot in the pit of my stomach when I woke up each day that stayed with me until I fell into a restless sleep each night. And I was very angry. I called it hurt, but the Lord looked right through my phony label, confronting me with the reality that I hated those people. I hated them for the things they had said about Dan. I hated them for betraying us. I hated them for not believing in us. I hated them for their deception and lies. God had nailed it. I hated them and had no clue how to deal with such a powerful emotion. So I did nothing…for a while.

One morning I was getting ready to run errands. I was reviewing the list of offenses I had collected over the past few months, feeding the fury raging in my heart. All of a sudden, Danna came rushing into the room to show me the beautiful house she had built with her Legos. As she rounded the corner, she tripped and fell. The house crumbled into a hundred pieces as it hit the tile floor. She looked up at me for assurance and asked, "Does it matter, Mama?" I said, "No, honey. It doesn't matter. I will help you build another house…a bigger and even better house."

The Lord stopped me in my tracks when I heard His tender voice whisper, "Exactly." And in that moment, sitting on the bathroom floor beside my little girl, I began to cry out all of the anger and pain, facing every ugly emotion that had been bottled up for months. Danna lingered quietly beside me on holy ground that had suddenly become an altar. I brought my offering of wounds and received healing in return. What an awesome God we serve. He has been true to His promise. He has indeed built a bigger and better house…in my life and in the life of Flamingo Road Church.

We cannot deal with negative emotions until we face them honestly and call them what they really are. When we do, healing begins. To identify our emotions, we must recognize the source from which they come and then label them correctly.

## Step Two: Harness Your Emotions

"A fool vents all his feelings, but a wise man holds them back"(Proverbs 29:11 nkjv). The Hebrew word used here for "holds them back" is the word "harness." The noun form of that verb literally means "straps and buckles." It is the picture of imprisonment and bondage. The verb form of "harness" means "to equip for work." Our emotions can either be a prison of bondage or an instrument of power. We can put them to work in our lives by taking two actions.

### Control Your Emotions

The word "harness" carries the idea of a bit in the mouth, a taking hold of the reins. Many times we allow our emotions to run wild, like stampeding horses. We must learn how to keep the reins of our emotions firmly in hand. That means that we must constantly choose to surrender them to the supernatural control of God. When we do, the Holy Spirit empowers that choice and produces a supernatural control within us. "The mind controlled by the Spirit is life and peace" (Romans 8:6).

> *Emotions can be stepping-*
> *stones or quicksand.*

My son is a very easygoing guy, but he also has a very big temper. It takes a lot to make him lose it. That is where his sister comes in. Danna is a party looking for a place to happen. She is full of life and intensity. When they were younger, there was a certain stretch of life where Danna was really pushing Jered's emotional buttons. Jered began to have trouble controlling his anger. So we invented the mad board. Dan took a piece of scrap wood and covered the entire surface with nails driven in halfway. We then told Jered that whenever he became angry and felt like hitting something or someone, he should go to the garage, grab his hammer, and pound away at the nails. It worked. And Jered learned he could handle his anger in a positive way, without the shedding of blood.

We all need a mad board in our lives. It may be a drive around the block or a long walk. It may be cleaning house or punching a boxing bag. It may be getting alone with God and pouring it all out. God will provide a mad board when you choose to control your emotions.

### Use Your Emotions

Emotions can be stepping-stones or quicksand. It all depends upon how we use them and invest our emotional energy. Jesus models for us how to use emotions in the right way. When He was in the temple and discovered that the moneychangers were violating His Father's house, He was furious. Scripture tells us that He stepped aside and braided a whip (John 2:15). Why? It was not because He was practicing a new braiding technique. I think He was angry and knew He needed a few minutes to harness that emotion. Once His anger was under control, once it was harnessed, Jesus used it to correct a wrong.

Jesus began His victorious journey to the cross in the Garden of Gethsemane. Mark 14 shows us it was there that He harnessed His fear. That harnessed fear was transformed into endurance. And that endurance produced joy. "Let us fix our eyes on Jesus, the author and perfecter of our faith, who for the joy set before him endured the cross" (Hebrews 12:2).

We choose where to invest our emotional energy. Like Jesus, we need to harness our emotions, using them as stepping stones from bad to good.

In the first two chapters, I shared in great detail about my struggle with clinical depression. It was the darkest time of my life. It was frightening and horrible. But I would go through it all again tomorrow for what He accomplished in my life through it. It has become the foundation upon which He has built a new life and identity. The most powerful and rewarding ministry of my life has flowed out of that slimy pit. I have been set free from many fears and false truths that had weighed me down for so long. His presence is more real and His power more evident. He has set that darkness around my life as a hedge of protection, an alarm system. When I feel myself slipping back into old patterns, drifting dangerously close to the edge of that all too familiar pit, I know it is time to stop. Something is wrong. My life is out of balance somewhere. My experience in the darkness has also opened up a whole new area of ministry to others who find themselves in a battle with depression. You cannot lead where you have not been. It takes a pit dweller to understand another pit dweller.

"He put a new song in my mouth. It was a song of praise to our God. Many people will see this and worship him. Then they will trust the LORD" (Psalm 40:3 ICB).

God has used the darkness of depression not only for my good but also for the good of others. That "new song of praise" was composed so that others might hear of His deliverance. To harness your emotions, take control of them and then use them.

## STEP THREE: BALANCE YOUR EMOTIONS

Emotional health is like a bank account. The withdrawals and deposits determine the balance. In order to have a balanced life, we must balance our emotions as well.

### Be Aware of Emotional Withdrawals

Emotional withdrawals were mentioned a little earlier. And many of them are good and right. Many are healthy and ordained. Several years ago, Dan and I had a friend who was the pastor of a fast-growing church. One day this young man showed up at our front door to tell us his wife was divorcing him. He lost his church, his wife, and his hope in one blow. For weeks and months we spent hours with this broken young man. He was in our home frequently and Dan talked with him by phone daily, even when we were out of town on vacation. Was this an emotional withdrawal for Dan and me? Absolutely. But it was also replenishing to invest time and love in this special relationship. Today this man is happily married, the father of two beautiful children, and a pastor serving a growing church. I believe our time with him was an emotional withdrawal with great dividends.

There are, however, emotional withdrawals that are not good and right. They are far from healthy and certainly not ordained by God. A woman named Sue walked into our church one day. She was a prostitute, a drug addict, and an alcoholic. She had done everything there was to do on the streets of Fort Lauderdale in order to support her hellish lifestyle. We led her to Christ and began to help her build a new life. It was then that I decided to disciple her. For months I spent hour after hour with her introducing her to the Bible and explaining what it meant to have a personal relationship with God. I became the one she wanted to please. I became the one who confronted the sin in her life. I became her savior. And let me tell you, I make a lousy savior. There was little growth in Sue's life, and she became totally dependent upon me for every spiritual need.

It was my daughter's words that God used to yank my eyes open. While Danna and I were waiting for Sue to arrive at our house for our weekly Bible study, she quietly asked, "Mama, why do you spend more time with Sue than you do with me?" My heart sank. I tried to recover with the explanation, "Honey, Sue is a baby Christian and I am trying to help her." Danna looked thoughtful for a moment and then walked away, leaving me with this indictment: "I don't think it's doing much good." And she was right. That day I turned Sue loose to the Savior who could really do something with her. And an amazing thing happened, Sue's life began to change, and she began to really grow in Christ. Soon she was depending on God instead of depending on me.

We have a limited supply of emotional resources. We must be careful to invest them in the places where it counts the most and will make the greatest difference. Some people are emotional black holes. The enemy will send an abundance of these draining people to you in order to keep you busy and exhausted, creating an emotional imbalance. Choose carefully where you invest your emotional energy.

## Make Consistent Emotional Deposits

It is not enough to guard the emotional withdrawals in our lives. We must make consistent emotional deposits in order to have a healthy emotional balance.

The greatest emotional deposit that we can make is to saturate our lives with the Word of God. It is powerful and life changing. It will give guidance and comfort, wisdom and strength, and become the "stack pole" of your emotional health.

One day Dan asked me to take our family van in for new tires. As I drove onto the service lot, I saw hundreds of tires lying everywhere. It was a mess. I left the van and walked across the street to have lunch while the tires were installed. When I returned, I was surprised to see a neat and orderly lot. I asked the manager what on earth he had done with all of the tires. He pointed into the garage, where I saw the tires neatly arranged by size. They had taken a large tire, filled the center with cement, and placed a metal pole in it. When the cement had dried, the workers slipped the tires over the pole, creating a neat stack. The Word of God brings our emotions into a healthy order. It becomes the stack pole for our emotions.

Another emotional deposit is prayer. A consistent and effective prayer life stabilizes us emotionally, as does solitude. Time alone and in prayer allows God to renew your spirit and unclutter your mind.

Replenishing relationships are a wonderful emotional deposit, and we need to make sure that our main friendships are with those who replenish us. There are some people who will suck the life right out of you and leave you emotionally empty. We must balance those draining relationships with others who pour life into the friendship.

Laughter and fun deposit pure energy into our emotional bank accounts. Have you ever noticed how good it feels to laugh? I mean, really laugh: the doubled over, tears running down the face, stomach cramping kind of laugh. My sister-in-law and her husband vacationed in North Carolina one summer and came home with a great present for me. It is a five-foot wooden sign that says, "Live well, laugh often, love much." What great advice.

We all know about bounced checks, don't we? Checks bounce when our bank account has insufficient funds. We have made too many withdrawals and not enough deposits. The same is true of our emotional lives. We must continually make enough deposits so that the withdrawals don't create an emotional bankruptcy.

A word of warning...if you are presented with the opportunity to serve, check the balance in your emotional account before you say yes. Ephesians 2:10 reminds us that "God has made us what we are. In Christ Jesus, God made us to do good works, which God planned in advance for us to live our lives doing" (NCV). The most effective ministry flows from a life in which the deposits outweigh the withdrawals.

## STEP FOUR: DISMISS UNHEALTHY EMOTIONS

Do you remember the country song that says, "You got to

know when to hold 'em, know when to fold 'em"? There is some truth in those words. Sometimes we need to quit holding on to an emotion and dismiss it. We need to release the anger, the hurt, or the fear that has been holding us back. We need to cut it loose from our hearts and let it go.

There are two important steps we can take to dismiss emotions in our lives that are not worth the emotional energy they require.

### Take Charge of Your Spirit

First, you must take charge of your spirit. This truth is illustrated in Psalm 103:1-2 where David is telling his spirit what to do. "Praise the LORD, O my soul; all my inmost being, praise his holy name. Praise the LORD, O my soul, and forget not all his benefits." David literally instructs his soul to praise God. He doesn't wait until he feels like praising God. He simply takes charge of his spirit and commands it to give God praise. David is being obedient and teaching the truth that emotional wholeness follows spiritual obedience. To take charge indicates a choice of will, a deliberate action.

Many times we don't want to let go of that negative emotion because we are afraid. The pain has become familiar. It defines who we are. Jesus asked the man at the pool, "Do you want to be healed?" (John 5:6 RSV). I always wondered why Jesus asked such a strange question. The man had been sick so long that his whole identity was wrapped around his illness. Who would he be apart from that illness? Sometimes it is easier to stay in the dark than to struggle toward the light. Maybe that is because the dark has become so familiar. It has become all we know. It becomes easier to stay where we are. Paralysis sets in. But Jesus is calling us to emotional wholeness by taking charge of our spirit.

### Guard Your Mind

Second, to dismiss negative emotions requires that we guard our minds. A powerful directive is given to us in 2 Corinthians 10:4-5:

> The weapons we fight with are not the weapons of the world. On the contrary, they have divine power to demolish strongholds. We demolish arguments and every pretension that sets itself up against the knowledge of God, and we take captive every thought to make it obedient to Christ.

We will have to guard our minds against negative emotions. "Take captive" is a military term painting the picture of a guard standing watch. Someone has to station the guard at the doorway of our minds. That means a choice must be made. The mind can become a breeding ground for negative emotions if we are not diligent in guarding its entryway.

We live in an area where large ships are constantly docking. They come and go from ports all around the world. When one comes into the port an inspection team is sent on board to determine if there is contamination of any kind. If there is, the ship and all of its contents are quarantined until it is cleaned up. Then another inspection team is sent to inspect the ship a second time. If it is free of contamination, then, and only then, is the ship given permission to dock. We need to guard our minds, examining every thought and emotion, and dismiss anything that tries to contaminate our lives.

God wants us to be healthy emotionally. That can only happen when we surrender ourselves to Him and learn, through His power, to manage our emotions.

# 9

# Getting Good
## *at* Being You

DEPRESSION OFTEN GROWS OUT OF a wrong perception of who we really are. We waste valuable energy and emotional strength performing, trying to earn the approval of those
we deem important. We search for love but find it impossible
to understand what anyone could see in us that is lovable. We
set unrealistic expectations and goals, hoping our perfectionist
efforts will cause someone to see us as a success. It is an exercise
in futility and soon we give up, settling for the life of failure we
knew we deserved all along. The pit of darkness is only a step
away. The darkness is almost a relief. At least the battle is over,
even if we are defeated.

Listen carefully. That is not God's plan for your life. He created
you with a special plan in mind. He loves you and wants you to
see yourself as He sees you, through the eyes of an unconditional
and transforming love.

A man paid a visit to his local psychologist. The doctor asked
what had prompted the visit. The man said, "I'm suffering from an

inferiority complex." For weeks the doctor ran a battery of tests. When he had compiled the results, he called the man in for the diagnosis. The doctor said, "I have some good news and some bad news. The good news is that you do not have an inferiority complex. The bad news is…you really are inferior."

Many of us are just like that man. It's been said, "No one can make you feel inferior without your permission." But many of us have allowed others to assign an identity to us that is false and untrue. That identity has become a prison. It has paralyzed us.

I have good news. You can discover who you really are. You can discover why you are here. You can be all that you were created to be. In short, God wants you to get good at being you.

> On a Sabbath Jesus was teaching in one of the synagogues, and a woman was there who had been crippled by a spirit for eighteen years. She was bent over and could not straighten up at all. When Jesus saw her, he called her forward and said to her, "Woman, you are set free from your infirmity." Then he put his hands on her, and immediately she straightened up and praised God. Indignant because Jesus had healed on the Sabbath, the synagogue ruler said to the people, "There are six days for work. So come and be healed on those days, not on the Sabbath." The Lord answered him, "You hypocrites. Doesn't each of you on the Sabbath untie his ox or donkey from the stall and lead it out to give it water? Then should not this woman, a daughter of Abraham, whom Satan has kept bound for eighteen long years, be set free on the Sabbath day from what bound her?" When he said this, all his opponents were humiliated, but the people were delighted with all the wonderful things he was doing (Luke 13:10-17).

We can learn to accept God's evaluation of us. We can learn to see ourselves as He sees us. We can learn to let His love and mercy free us from those things that bind us. He stands waiting for us to come to Him so that He can make us all we are meant to be.

## STEP ONE: REALIZE THAT JESUS KNOWS YOU AND STILL LOVES YOU

"When Jesus saw her, he called her forward and said to her, 'Woman, you are set free from your infirmity'" (Luke 13:12). Jesus knew this woman. He looked past her pain into the depths of her being and saw who she really was and all that she was created to be. He could have called her by name, but He said, "woman." He included her whole identity in that name; everything she was at that moment, everything she had been in the past, everything she hoped to be in the future. He knew every detail of her life, and He loved her. We find the assurance of His concern for us in Matthew 10:30: "Even the very hairs of your head are all numbered."

*Your identity was established before the world began, in the heart and mind of God.*

This woman had been assigned an identity by the relentless illness that plagued her body. Anyone who knew her identified her by that illness. Her heart must have been filled with feelings of unworthiness. I imagine she felt unwanted and unloved. She must have felt like a nobody. But when Jesus saw her, He looked at her through different eyes and called her to Himself. With one word from Him, everything changed and would never be the same again. All of a sudden, she was somebody.

There she stood, sick and in pain to the point that she was completely doubled over. Imagine what she felt when she realized that Jesus was talking to her. He was calling her, an outcast. And when she heard His voice, she heard something she hadn't heard for a very long time, if ever. She heard the unfamiliar but longed-for voice of love.

Many of us feel unwanted. Many of us feel unloved. We can rest assured that God knows us and loves us just as we are, right where we are in the midst of our mess and sickness. Listen! He is calling your name. One of my favorite verses of Scripture is Jeremiah 1:5: "Before I formed you in the womb I knew you, before you were born I set you apart."

Your identity was established before the world began, in the heart and mind of God. Before you were wanted or not wanted by human hearts, before you were planned or not planned by human minds, you were wanted and planned in the heart and mind of God. Created by God…for God. Wow! That makes you important. You are valuable—and the simple but almost unbelievable reason is that God created you.

You can judge a product's worth and value by looking at the one who made it. I was recently reminded of this truth when I went to buy a new sofa. Our old one was truly pathetic. I had a garage sale and made enough profit for a trip to the furniture outlet. I walked in with a certain amount of money to spend and a definite idea of what I wanted, so I avoided the salesmen and began my search. I narrowed the choice down to two sofas. Both were in my price range and both would work in my living room. Out of the corner of my eye, I saw a salesman making a bee-line for me, sensing a sale in the air. Before he could say a word, I whirled around and asked, "If I were your wife, which one of these would you tell me to buy?" Without a moment's hesitation he pointed to one of the sofas. Curious, I said, "Why did you choose that one?" He shrugged his shoulders and replied, "Easy. That one is a trusted brand name you will recognize and is made with quality. The other one is just a cheap imitation. You should always check the label."

Take a look at your label found in Psalm 139:13-16:

> For you created my inmost being; you knit me together in my mother's womb. I praise you because I am fearfully and wonderfully made; your works are wonderful; I know that full well. My frame was not hidden from you when I was made in the secret place. When I was woven together in the depths of the earth, your eyes saw my unformed body. All the days ordained for me were written in your book before one of them came to be.

Getting good at being you recognizes the truth that He knows you and loves you.

## STEP TWO: LEAVE SOME THINGS BEHIND

Jesus could certainly have healed the woman from Luke 13 right where she stood. Instead, "when Jesus saw her, he called her forward" (verse 12). There must have been a reason. I believe Jesus wanted her to leave some things behind. When He called her, she had a choice to make. She could choose to stay where she was, in the darkness that had been home for so long. That didn't seem like a great option. Or she could choose to lay down the weight of her struggle and come to a Savior with love in His eyes and hope in His hand, offering a new beginning, a new identity in Him. Her healing began when she took the first step. It was a step of faith and obedience. She laid down everything in her life and stepped toward healing, exchanging her prison for freedom, darkness for light.

I admire people who run marathons. I have several friends who jog frequently and really enjoy the thrill of a race. I am a very good sideline cheerleader. Imagine with me a race where every runner shows up in their best running attire and lines up at the starting line. One last runner joins the crowd. He is dressed in a business suit covered by a raincoat, just in case a storm blows in. On his feet are heavy work boots, and an umbrella hangs around his neck. In one hand he is carrying a lunch box, and in the other is a water bottle. His pockets are filled with Tylenol, BenGay, Band-Aids, and Pepto-Bismol. How is he going to run the race?

Ridiculous, isn't it? And yet we try to live life weighed down by many things that hinder us in the race. Hebrews 12:1 tells us to "lay aside every weight, and the sin which so easily ensnares us, and let us run with endurance the race that is set before us" (NKJV). What are some of the weights we need to lay down?

## The Weight of the Past

This woman had to be willing to lay down her past and come to Jesus in faith. We can allow our past to defeat us or we can harness it and use it for power in our lives today. There really is only one healthy choice: We must deal with it and then walk on. Paul put it this way: "One thing I do: Forgetting what is behind and straining toward what is ahead, I press on toward the goal to win the prize for which God has called me heavenward in Christ Jesus" (Philippians 3:13-14). We need to live life straining toward the prize. To get good at being you, forget what was and press on toward what can be.

## The Weight of Sin

We need to keep short books on sin. When we allow sin to build in our lives, it brings a sense of condemnation. Guilt is given a foothold and begins its destructive work. But God has a plan for our sin. Isaiah 1:18 promises, "Though your sins are like scarlet, they shall be as white as snow; though they are red as crimson, they shall be like wool." In Psalm 103:12 we find that "as far as the east is from the west, so far has he removed our transgression from us."

Some years ago, Dan and I went to Washington, D.C., to lead a youth revival in a Korean church. At the end of the week a lady from the church invited us out to dinner. We went to a wonderful but very expensive restaurant. At the end of the meal, she went to pay the bill. I saw her talking with the restaurant owner, and I could tell she was upset. I was afraid she did not have enough money, but when she came back to the table her explanation amazed me. She said that someone from the church had come in, seen us all eating together, and paid the bill. She was upset because she did not have the honor of paying for our meal. The manager apologized but said he could not accept any payment from her because someone else had already paid the bill.

We keep trying to pay for our sin when all we need to do is accept His forgiveness for it and leave it behind.

## The Weight of Good Things

Some of us need to leave some things behind that are good. Good things can be distractions from the best things. We can be busy doing good things and miss the highest things for our lives. The story of Mary and Martha in Luke 10 illustrates this truth. Martha was so busy serving that she missed the opportunity to enjoy Jesus being in her house. But her sister Mary took the time to sit at His feet. Sometimes the good things we are so busy doing can keep us from the best things that are vital.

## STEP THREE: KEEP A DREAM IN YOUR HEART

"On a Sabbath Jesus was teaching in one of the synagogues,

and a woman was there who had been crippled by a spirit for eighteen years" (Luke 13:10-11). This woman had every reason to give up on God. But where do we find her? She is in the synagogue. I'm sure news about Jesus had come to her city. I imagine she had tried every remedy anyone had suggested. Nothing had worked. But maybe this time...

She was still searching for freedom. She kept hoping and dreaming. It was the dream that gave her strength to keep walking straight through her fears and doubts, right into the arms of God and His plan. So many of us are without hope and dreams because we are living our plan, not His. He is the maker of dreams, and He has a plan for every problem. That plan may be deliverance from the problem. That plan may be deliverance in the problem. Either way, His plan is good. "'For I know the plans I have for you,' declares the LORD, 'plans to prosper you and not to harm you, plans to give you hope and a future'" (Jeremiah 29:11).

How do we find that plan? We must start by reading the Plan Book. Last year when my son was in the middle of summer football practice, he left early one morning looking forward to their first real scrimmage. He came home, drenched in sweat and disgusted with some of his teammates. When I asked why, he said that because they had not studied the playbook and didn't know their running routes, the practice had been a total disaster. It is amazing to me that we wonder about the disasters in our lives when we have not studied the Plan Book and, as a result, don't know which routes to take. Plug the Word of God into your life on a consistent basis and watch the plan unfold.

Prayer is a major part of finding God's plan for our lives. God wants to show you His plan for your life even more than you want to know the plan. Ask Him. Spend time on your knees and the plan will come.

A mission statement is also helpful in discovering His plan. After praying and filling your life with His truth, sit down and ask God to show you His mission for your life. Ask yourself these questions:

- What is the center of my life?
- What five things do I want to accomplish in my life?
- What am I doing that will count for eternity?
- Where can I invest my time and energy so that they will have the greatest impact?
- What "God-sized" dream am I dreaming right now?

I dreamed of ministering to hurting women. Today, I have the opportunity to travel all across North and South America, teaching and sharing my journey with others. The Lord has given me a tape ministry, and you hold in your hands my first book. All of these were God-sized dreams.

The best part of you has a dream. Don't be afraid to dream it. Don't be afraid to live it. And if one dream has died, dream another. Keep a dream in your heart.

## Step Four: Don't Waste Your Pain

God uses broken people. He can shine best through broken people and is, in fact, drawn to those who are broken. Ernest Hemingway puts it this way in *A Farewell to Arms:* "The world breaks everyone and many are strong at the broken places."

Jesus looked out over the crowd that day the crippled woman came to worship. There were probably many women there. Jesus knew every one of them. If I had been in His place and had to choose someone, I would have chosen a winner. I am thankful for His choice. He could have chosen the most beautiful or the most talented, but He chose the most broken. She had refused to waste her pain, and it became a highway that led straight to Jesus. Your pain can lead you to Him too.

Paul reminds us that we live in "jars of clay to show that this all-surpassing power is from God and not from us" (2 Corinthians 4:7). God has always used broken vessels to accomplish His greatest work. He even wrapped up His perfect Son in a jar of clay and then used Him to change the world.

Don't waste your pain. God doesn't. He is aware of your heartaches. He knows what you are feeling. You thought no one understood. You thought no one heard you crying in the darkness of that pit. But He does. "You have collected all my tears in your bottle. You have recorded every one in your book" (Psalm 56:8 NLT).

Pain comes to us with His permission. There is a purpose in every pain. C.S. Lewis said that "God whispers in our pleasures, speaks in our conscience, shouts in our pain." As Barbara Johnson says, "Pain is inevitable but misery is optional."

Pain carries with it a choice:

- a choice in attitude
- a choice in direction
- a choice of victory or defeat
- a choice of bitterness or sweetness

What have you done with your pain?

Dan has coached our kids in soccer for several years. During one game, Danna was elbowed in the chest by a boy on the other team and came to the sideline in tears. Dan was comforting her and trying to calm her down. Through clenched teeth, she said, "I'm gonna go back in there and punch his lights out." That sounded like a good plan to me. Fortunately, her father did not agree and asked her a question. "Danna, do you really want to get him?" Boy, did she. "Let me tell you how. The score is tied and there are two minutes left in the game. Go back in there, defend your spot, and help us win." She went back in, and with

30 seconds left to play, our team scored the winning goal. Danna learned you can use your pain for good.

Ask yourself these questions:

- What lesson have I learned?
- Has it made me stronger?
- Has it made me more sensitive to the hurt of others?
- Has it changed the direction of my life?
- Has it brought healing?
- Has it made me cry out to God?
- Has it made me grow?

Oswald Chambers said, "Why does God bring thunderclouds and disasters when we want green pastures and still waters? Bit by bit we find, behind the clouds, the Father's feet; behind the lightning, an abiding day that has no night; behind the thunder, a still, small voice that comforts with a comfort that is unspeakable." Don't waste your pain.

## STEP FIVE: BE PATIENT

This crippled woman had been sick for 18 long years. Talk about patience! My prayer for patience usually goes something like this: "Dear God, please make me more patient, and would You please hurry?" I heard about a young Christian who went to an older believer, asking for prayer. "Will you please pray that I will be more patient?" was his request. They knelt together and the older man began to pray. "Lord, send this young man trouble in the morning. Send him more trouble in the afternoon. And in the evening…" At that point, the young Christian blurted out, "No! You misunderstood. I didn't want you to pray for trouble. I wanted you to pray for patience." The wise old man replied, "You don't understand. It is through trouble that we learn patience."

> *It is impossible to have a real encounter with the living God and not be changed.*

To become what God wants us to be takes time and trouble. Pruning is painful but necessary for growth. "God began doing a good work in you. And He will continue it until it is finished" (Philippians 1:6 ICB). Sometimes we can't see Him working and grow impatient. It is during those times that we need to listen carefully for His voice.

This woman was doubled over. She could not see Him, but she could hear Him. I love the song that says, "When you can't see His hand, trust His heart." What a great truth. Be patient. He'll make you all that you are supposed to be. Oswald Chambers said that "God engineers our circumstances as He did those of His Son; all we have to do is to follow where He places us. The majority of us are busy trying to place ourselves. God alters things while we wait for Him." Be patient. He is not finished yet.

## STEP SIX: PRACTICE PRAISE

"Then he put his hands on her, and immediately she straightened up and praised God" (Luke 13:13). It is impossible to have a real encounter with the living God and not be changed. When we encounter God, when He touches our lives, when we discover who God wants us to be, we will praise Him. We were created to praise Him. "Let every created thing give praise to the LORD" (Psalm 148:5 NLT).

Many times we feel we have nothing to celebrate. We do not understand the true meaning of praise. Praise comes from a Latin word that means "value" or "worth." So to praise God means to celebrate His worth, His value…His presence. "Sing to God, sing praise to his name, extol him who rides on the clouds—his name is the LORD—and rejoice before him" (Psalm 68:4).

Praise is not optional. Praise is essential. It is a demonstration of trust and the acceptance of a circumstance without insisting that He change it. When we are praising God, we are trusting Him and walking in obedience.

Fanny Crosby lost her sight in infancy because a doctor applied the wrong medicine to her eyes. She had a choice. She could have become bitter and filled with anger. She chose instead to praise God and spent her life writing the words to more than 8000 praise songs. Miss Crosby demonstrated the truth that the highest act of praise is to be what God made us to be. Let's practice praise.

## STEP SEVEN: REACH OUT TO OTHERS

Luke 13:12 implies an important truth in discovering who we are: "When Jesus saw her, he called her forward and said to her, 'Woman, you are set free from your infirmity.' "

Freedom has a responsibility. When we are set free, we must show others where they can find the same freedom.

> All praise to the God and Father of our Master, Jesus the Messiah! Father of all mercy! God of all healing counsel! He comes alongside us when we go through hard times, and before you know it, he brings us alongside someone else who is going through hard times so that we can be there for that person just as God was there for us (2 Corinthians 1:3-4 THE MESSAGE).

Geese don't have a great reputation. They are fairly dull and ordinary in comparison to other birds. They are really noticed only once a year when they migrate. Then it is easy to see that they are a precision flying team that, together, can fly 70 percent longer than when they fly alone. A lead goose cuts a path through the air resistance, which creates uplift for the two birds behind him. Also, his beating wings make it easier on the birds behind him. Each bird takes his turn at being the leader. The tired ones fan out to the edges of the "V" for a breather. The rested ones move toward the point of the "V". If a goose is too tired or sick and has to drop out of the flock, it is never abandoned. A stronger goose stays with the weaker one until it is well enough to fly again.

If geese are wise enough to reach out and help each other, surely we can figure out how to do the same.

## A Final Thought

When Hurricane Andrew roared through our area, we had little damage compared to so many others. We did, however, lose a few large trees. One tree in the front yard was partially destroyed, and everyone who saw it advised us to cut it down. They said it was too damaged and would never be any good again. But Dan loves a challenge. He saw something in that tree no one else could see. He propped the tree up with wooden reinforcements and cut off the dead limbs.

Today, if you drive by that house, the fullest and most beautiful tree in the yard is the tree that everyone said was no good. The tree that would not have made it without some serious support is thriving.

Jesus sees something in you no one else can see. And He wants to empower you today to begin the journey of getting good at being you.

# 10

# Making Friends

FRIENDSHIP IS THE BASIS OF every healthy relationship. We all need friends, and we all need to learn how to be a friend. People without healthy friendships are much more likely to experience depression. The person who is struggling with depression needs a strong support team of friends.

I walked into the pit of depression alone, with few friendships. I had married my best friend. But I soon realized that it was wrong to expect Dan to meet all of my emotional needs. I isolated myself with my pain, sharing it with no one except him. The darkness is a very frightening place when you are alone. Yet there were many people who would have stepped into my life as a friend if I had let them.

Sitting in the darkness, I longed for a true friend, a soul mate with whom I could truly be myself. I slowly began to realize that to have that kind of friend, I would have to be that kind of friend. I had no idea where to start. God began to gently guide me into His truth about the importance of friends.

Some random thoughts about friendship floated through that pit:

- When you're in a jam, good friends will bring you bread with peanut butter on it.
- A friend is one who knows all about you and loves you anyway.
- Message in a fortune cookie: "You appeal to a small select group of confused people."
- A friend is: a push when you've stopped, a word when you're lonely, a guide when you're searching, a smile when you're sad, a song when you're glad.
- A friend will joyfully sing with you when you are on the mountaintop, and silently walk beside you through the valley.

Friendship is the launching pad for every love in life and the foundation of all healthy relationships. In his book, *The Broken Heart: The Medical Consequences of Loneliness,* Dr. James J. Lynch shows that lonely people live significantly shorter lives than the general population. It is a simple fact that we need each other. We need friends.

There are many different levels of friendships. There are friends we see occasionally. There are friends with whom we share the important things in life. Then there are friends with whom we share every tiny detail. All of these friendships are necessary and good.

It is important to understand that there are also seasons of friendships. Friendships will sometimes change with the seasons of our lives. But we still need friends, and we will always need different kinds of friendships.

One of the most beautiful portraits of friendship in the Bible is found in the book of Ruth. It is the story of Naomi, a godly woman. She was married, had two married sons, and was living in the land of Moab. There Naomi's husband and both sons died, leaving three women alone, Naomi and her daughters-in-law, Ruth and Orpah. Because they had no food or money, Naomi wanted to return to Bethlehem, her homeland.

On the way to Bethlehem, Naomi stopped and told Ruth and Orpah that they should return to their homes, because there they will have the opportunity to marry again and start new lives. Ruth and Orpah objected, but Naomi was unrelenting. Can't you just see this scene: all three of these women, standing in the middle of the road, in tears.

Orpah kissed Naomi goodbye and returned home, but Ruth absolutely refused to leave Naomi. Naomi was more than a mother-in-law to Ruth. She was her friend.

> But Ruth replied, "Don't urge me to leave you or to turn back from you. Where you go I will go, and where you stay I will stay. Your people will be my people and your God my God. Where you die I will die, and there I will be buried. May the LORD deal with me, be it ever so severely, if anything but death separates you and me." When Naomi realized that Ruth was determined to go with her, she stopped urging her (Ruth 1:16-18).

Naomi was astonished at the love and loyalty of Ruth. So together Ruth and Naomi traveled to Bethlehem and began a new life. It was in Bethlehem that Ruth met a young man named Boaz. They were married and had a son who later became the grandfather of King David.

*True friendship takes time.*

Just think about it. Ruth, a Gentile from a foreign country, became part of the family line of Jesus Christ, the Son of God. Why? Because Ruth was loyal. Because Ruth was a friend. Wouldn't you like to have a friend like that? Wouldn't you like to be a friend like that?

This precious story of friendship offers us several keys that will unlock the secret of healthy friendships.

## KEY ONE: TIME

Ruth promised, "Where you go I will go. Where you stay I will stay" (Ruth 1:16). She was willing to commit her life in friendship to Naomi. Emerson wrote, "We take care of our health, we lay up money, we make our rooms tight and our clothing sufficient, but who provides wisely that he shall not be wanting in the best property of all—friends?"

True friendship takes time. Friendship takes cultivation, attention, and prioritizing the relationship. Friendship doesn't just happen and will not be dropped on our front doorstep by the mailman. We have to develop a lifestyle that allows us to dispense time in friendship. Time spent together in friendship creates a "memory bank." From that bank we can make withdrawals when we are running low. Time is a priceless gift and a powerful communicator of love. When you give 30 minutes of time, you are giving 30 minutes of life. That gift of time takes planning and often a sacrifice of your own agenda.

Ruth was willing to sacrifice not only her own agenda for the present, but like a precious gift, she set aside her whole future for the sake of a friendship. In a "quick-fix" world we need to realize that friendship takes time. The depth of that friendship depends upon how much time we can and are willing to invest.

In a previous chapter, I mentioned my friend Michelle Johnson. She is the perfect example of someone who is willing to invest time in friendship. When I first shared my depression with Michelle, she immediately made a choice about her role in my life. She did not wait for me to ask for her help. She did not pause to count the cost of being my friend. She simply stepped whole-heartedly into my life and began to walk with me through that ugly, slimy pit. She bought groceries. She picked up my cleaning. She listened for hours as I talked about everything—and nothing. She prayed and cried with me. She made me laugh and fussed at me like a mother hen. Today, her friendship is beyond measure in my life—because of the time she invested in me.

## KEY TWO: RISK

Ruth was willing to risk her very future to be loyal to Naomi. I have come to realize there is no love without risk. "Greater love has no one than this, that one lay down his life for his friends" (John 15:13 NASB). When you lay down your life, you take a chance on being rejected and hurt. At times you may be misunderstood and even betrayed.

I do not have a green thumb, but I once had a neighbor in Clinton, Mississippi, who did. She grew the most beautiful roses I had ever seen. They spilled over our fence in a rainbow of colors: pink, yellow, red, and white. In the afternoons when my kids woke up from their naps, we would head to the backyard where they played and I visited with my neighbor. She always wore heavy, thick gloves when working the rose bed because of the spiny thorns. But occasionally she would remove the gloves and show me where a thorn had left its mark, even through the gloves. One day, my son saw her "boo-boo" and asked her why she liked those nasty flowers that gave her a "shot." She laughed and asked Jered, "Do you think my flowers are pretty?" Jered answered, "Yes, they are very pretty." My neighbor explained, "I think so too. They are so pretty that they make me forget about the way they sometimes hurt my hands. I just try to be careful when I handle them so that I don't get too many hurts." Friendship is like that. It will bring hurt and an occasional wound. But the beauty of friendship is worth an occasional wound. If we handle the friendship carefully and with respect, the wounds will be few.

It is important to love and cherish our friends, but we can't hold our friends responsible for our happiness. Jesus Christ is the only friend who will never disappoint or hurt us. We need to expect that all others will. I have a friend who just cannot keep confidences. She would do anything for me, except keep her mouth shut. But because I love her and don't want to write her off as a friend, I have learned to simply be cautious about what I share. Every friendship involves a cost, a risk.

First Peter 4:8 says, "Love covers a multitude of sins." Love takes into account the flaws of human frailty. Love spreads itself over those flaws and chooses to love anyway. Friendship always involves risk.

## Key Three: Forgiveness

Naomi was Ruth's mother-in-law. Naomi was a woman who loved and served God. One of her sons had married Ruth, who did not worship God. Yet they loved each other deeply. Forgiveness had to be a part of this relationship. Forgiveness has to be part of every friendship.

Forgiveness is our responsibility. God takes care of healing the hurt. Colossians 3:13 commands us to "bear with each other and forgive whatever grievances you may have against one another. Forgive as the Lord forgave you." To bear with someone is to put up with them, to accept them and their flaws, loving them as is. And as if that's not enough, the verse goes on to tell us to do it the way Jesus did. That means to take the initiative in forgiving, to be quick to give and receive forgiveness.

Forgiveness is always a deliberate choice, a chosen attitude, a discipline of the heart and will. I love a quote from Clara Barton, the founder of the American Red Cross. It is a beautiful illustration of forgiveness at its best. A friend of Miss Barton once reminded her of an especially cruel act someone had done to her years before. But Miss Barton acted as though she did not recall the incident. "Don't you remember?" her friend asked. "No," replied Clara Barton. "I distinctly remember forgetting it." Good friendships practice forgiveness.

## KEY FOUR: TRANSPARENCY

Ruth demonstrates an amazing transparency when she says, "Where you go, I will go. Where you stay I will stay. Your people will be my people and your God, my God" (Ruth 1:16). Openness and honesty nourish friendship. We are drawn to people who are transparent because they are authentic. There are no surprises with them—no land mines.

One of the most engaging qualities of Jesus was that He lived in the midst of His disciples' lives. He ate with them, prayed with them, cried with them, laughed with them. Over and over He opened Himself up to them. We see this transparency in John 15:15: "I do not call you servants any longer, because the servant does not know what the master is doing; but I have called you friends, because I have made known to you everything that I have heard from my Father" (NRSV). Jesus made a deliberate choice to be transparent. Was He hurt...betrayed...rejected? Yes. But still today He waits to be the most transparent and authentic friend you have ever had. To be a friend, the walls must come down, the masks must be put away, and we must be willing to let people in.

Before going to Flamingo I had few close friends. But once we were there, Dan and I made a deliberate choice to be transparent. As a result of that choice, I had more friends than at any other time in my life. Was I hurt? Was I burned? Yes, I was. Was it worth it? Absolutely. Remember, the occasional wound is worth the beauty of a true friendship. Friendship requires transparency.

## KEY FIVE: TOUCH

Ruth 1:4 tells us that Naomi both kissed and clung to her daughters-in-law. Physical touch is a powerful communicator of love. If we could follow Jesus in His ministry, we would see this truth demonstrated. Matthew 8:3 tells us that Jesus "reached out his hand and touched the [leper]." In Mark 10:16 Jesus "took the children into his arms." He knew the power of physical touch.

In this world there are varying degrees of communication through touch. A hug, a pat on the back, a squeezed hand are all points of connection that can encourage and convey the powerful message of love. We must be sensitive to the comfort level of others and respect their emotional boundaries.

A group of medical students was receiving training in the children's ward of a large hospital. One particular student was especially loved by all of the children. When he walked in, their faces would light up. The other medical students could not understand why. One night they decided to follow him as he made his rounds. When he checked on the children during his final round, they found their answer. The young medical student kissed each child goodnight. Ephesians 2:14 talks about Jesus breaking down the walls that divide us. There are times when a wall can only be broken down with a hug, a hand on a shoulder, or a kiss on the cheek. Touch is a powerful key to friendship.

## KEY SIX: CORRECTION

Naomi told Ruth to return to her hometown. Ruth loved her too much to comply. "When Naomi realized that Ruth was determined to go with her, she stopped urging her" (Ruth 1:18). Healthy friendships must have the element of correction. A true friend puts your good above the risk of anger or rejection. Proverbs 27:6 is an unusual verse: "Faithful are the wounds of a friend" (NKJV). The wound is the correction or confrontation given out of love and concern. Silence is agreement. Sometimes silence is the same as quietly watching a friend walk toward a cliff. We must learn to confront in love. And the harder the truth, the more love we must use to say it. Correction should always be given gently and for the right reason. The right reason is always restoration. Renee and Sharon are two friends who are pros at this. They watch me like a hawk. If they sense that I am stressed or overcommitted, they are on the phone or at my house. They have no problem looking at me and saying, "Are you exercising every day? Are you too busy? You look tired. You are doing too much and need to slow down." I know they are my friends because they are willing to correct me in love.

*A healthy friendship can withstand change.*

## KEY SEVEN: FREEDOM

The healthiest friendships are those in which each person gives the other room to grow and change instead of insisting that they remain the same. "[Love] does not insist on its own way" (1 Corinthians 13:5 NRSV). The unique relationship Ruth and Naomi had certainly demonstrated this quality. Naomi was willing to let Ruth start a whole new life…without her. As they walked the road to Bethlehem, I'm sure they both felt very unsure of the future. They knew there would be changes, but neither woman knew what they would be or what they would require of them. A healthy friendship can withstand change. Notice that Naomi gave both of her daughters-in-law the freedom to leave. Ruth remained, but Orpah returned home. And when she did, Naomi did not criticize or condemn her decision to do so. If one person in a friendship changes, the whole relationship changes. Friendship should be knit together with an elastic material that will always allow and make room for growth and change. Friendship can easily be destroyed by jealousy because jealousy is born out of unrealistic expectations and a possessive spirit. Friends must give each other space and freedom.

## Key Eight: Loyalty

Ruth and Naomi were loyal to each other. Orpah went home and Ruth stayed. Scripture tells us that it was this very quality that attracted Boaz to Ruth. In Ruth 2:11, Boaz says, "I've been told all about what you have done for your mother-in-law since the death of your husband—how you left your father and mother and your homeland and came to live with a people you did not know before." He was impressed with Ruth and her loyalty.

Loyalty is one of the most important keys to a healthy friendship. Proverbs 17:17 tells us "a friend loves at all times." Do you know what "all" means in the original Hebrew? It means all. True friends are committed to each other all the time. Their commitment does not waver when the audience changes, times are hard, or even in the midst of conflict.

Here are some practical ways to demonstrate loyalty to your friends:

- never criticize them to others
- applaud their successes
- share their burdens
- accept them as they are

- pick them up when they fall
- always be willing to listen
- be their cheerleader

Guard your friendships with loyalty.

## KEY NINE: ACTION

Ruth demonstrated her love for Naomi not only by her words, but also by her actions. She went with her to Bethlehem. She worked in the field with her. The best friendships are created by multiple layers of kind actions. Words are good, but the proof is in the doing.

We are told in 1 John 3:18 that we must love "not in word or speech, but in truth and action" (NRSV). Here are some actions that you can take in friendship.

### Traditions

Traditions are one of the most important ingredients in solid friendships. It may be a weekly lunch or a daily coffee break, a special shopping trip to your favorite mall or dinner and a movie on the first Saturday of each month. The pastors' wives of our church try to have dinner together on a regular basis. We are so rowdy that we have almost been thrown out of several restaurants. We love to relish those moments. Traditions build memories that accumulate and encourage friendship.

My mother was a nurse. Every afternoon she would come home from work, change clothes, and hand wash her uniform at the kitchen sink. While she stood there, she would watch through the window over the sink for Mrs. Chism, our neighbor. Mrs. Chism, seeing mother at the sink, would walk across the empty lot that separated our house from hers, knock on the door and come in for a cold drink and a visit. It was a daily tradition that was part of their friendship.

## Gifts

Giving a gift is a wonderful action to take in friendship. This includes all kinds of gifts. The gift doesn't have to be big or expensive. It is simply a symbol of time, energy, and thought given to a friend. It could be a note or a funny card, a magnet for the refrigerator, or a favorite candy bar. The greatest gift that you can give to a friend is yourself. Favors done back and forth, errands run, or a phone call just to say "hi"—these are all tiny statements of love and are especially important in times of crisis.

I have a friend named Bonnie who lives in Brandon, Florida. We don't get to see each other very often, but we have been friends for 20 years. I love her and know that she loves me. Bonnie's dad had been very sick and was dying of cancer. A phone call came letting us know he only had hours to live. Bonnie, knowing our busy lives, did not ask us to come, but Dan and I both knew she needed us. We booked a flight for that afternoon. When we arrived, we quietly let ourselves into the house. We were sitting on the sofa when Bonnie walked in. I will never forget the look on her face or the words she spoke as she began to cry. "You will never, never know what this means to me," she said.

Sometimes hurting friends can't ask for help. When you sense a need, just meet it.

## Words

Ephesians 4:29 says, "Do not let any unwholesome talk come out of your mouths, but only what is helpful for building others up according to their needs, that it may benefit those who listen."

The words of a friend edify. We need to be careful with our criticism. It should always be spoken one-on-one, face-to-face.

On the other hand, we need to be free with our encouragement. And we not only need to speak it, we need to write it.

When my son was ten years old, he gave me a box for Mother's Day. He had built it himself and painted it blue. I keep that box in my bedroom in a special place, not only because Jered made it for me, but also because it serves an important purpose. Every note of encouragement I receive goes in the blue box. When I become discouraged or "blue," I pull a few of those notes out and read them. They never fail to cheer me up. First Thessalonians 5:11 tells us to "encourage one other and build each other up." The word "encourage" means to "inspire courage" or to "put courage in." Friends look for reasons in each other to praise God. They seize every opportunity to deposit some courage into the life of a friend. Friends shine a spotlight on the good qualities and minimize the bad.

The words of a real friend are sensitive. This is the idea of being "tuned in" to the feelings of your friend. It is being real and loving. Brenda is a friend like this. One Sunday Brenda and I passed each other on the stairs at church. We were both in a hurry and gave the typical greeting of "Hi there" and "How are you?" Brenda stopped in the middle of the stairway, looked at me, and said, "I can tell something is bothering you. Can I help?" We stepped into a corner and I shared the burden I thought was carefully hidden. She prayed for me and gave me a hug, and then we went our separate ways. The entire exchange lasted five minutes, but because of her sensitivity, I was encouraged to go on. Take time to be sensitive to the needs of a friend.

## Listening

Listening, by definition, means "attention, with the intention to understand." James 1:19 tells us that "everyone should be quick to listen, slow to speak." There is a reason we have two ears and only one mouth. We should listen twice as much as we talk.

Ruth and Naomi were great friends in part because they were great listeners. Ruth listened to her mother-in-law give advice. I do the same thing with my mother-in-law. I listen to everything she says—and then I make up my own mind!

Jesus was a remarkable listener. He constantly drew people out by asking questions. Sometimes the best thing a friend can do is to offer a listening ear and heart. Put away the sermon, hold onto your advice, and just listen.

## A Final Thought

We all need to learn how to be a friend. God did not create us to be islands, He created us to love each other. John 13:34-35 tells us why: "A new command I give you: Love one another. As I have loved you, so you must love one another. By this all men will know that you are my disciples, if you love one another." Does the world know we are His disciples by the way we love each other, by the way we relate to each other...by our friendships?

Little Chad was a shy, quiet boy. One day he came home and told his mother he'd like to make a valentine for everyone in his class. Her heart sank. She thought, "I wish he wouldn't do that." She had watched the children when they walked home from school. Her Chad was always behind them. They laughed and hung on to each other and talked to each other. But Chad was never included.

Chad's mother decided she would go along with her son. She purchased paper, glue, and crayons. For three whole weeks, night after night, Chad painstakingly made 35 valentines. Valentine's Day came and Chad was beside himself with excitement. He carefully stacked them up, put them in a bag, and bolted out the door. His mom decided to bake him his favorite cookies to eat when he came home from school. She just knew he would be disappointed—maybe that would ease the pain a little. It hurt her to think he wouldn't receive many valentines—maybe none at all. That afternoon she had the cookies and a glass of milk on the table. When she heard voices she looked out the window. Sure enough, here they came, laughing and having the best time. And, as always, there was Chad in the rear. But he was walking a little faster than usual. She fully expected him to burst into tears as soon as he was inside. His arms were empty, she noticed, and when the door opened, she choked back her own tears. "Mommy has some warm cookies and milk for you," she said. But he hardly heard her words. He just marched right on by, his face shining, and all he could say was: "Not a one—not a one." Her heart sank. And then he added, "I didn't forget a one, Mom, not a single one."

So it is when God is in control of our friendships.

# 11

# Learning *the* Secret *of* Contentment

ONCE UPON A TIME THERE was a farmer who had lived on the same farm all his life. It was a good farm, but with the passing years, the farmer began to tire of it and long for a change, for something "better." Every day he found something else wrong with his farm until he finally decided to sell. He listed the farm with a Realtor, who quickly made up a sales flier emphasizing the good points of the farm: ideal location, modern equipment, healthy stock, acres of fertile ground. But before she ran the ad she called the farmer and read it to him for his approval. The farmer listened as she read. When the Realtor had finished, the farmer cried out, "Hold everything! I have changed my mind. I'm not going to sell. I've been looking for a place like that all of my life."

Many of us are constantly looking for something "better." Deep in our hearts we long for something more. We are not content. And because depression flourishes in discontentment, we must learn how to find contentment in every day life. What is the secret of contentment?

To answer this question, we turn again to Paul, a man in the Bible who had every reason to be discontented. He wrote the book of Philippians from prison, where he was awaiting trial and facing execution. He was old, alone, and had been brutally beaten, even stoned, for his faith in Jesus Christ. His health was bad, and he was almost blind. And yet, through the darkness of his pain, he joyfully exclaims, "I have learned to be content in whatever circumstances I am" (Philippians 4:11 NASB).

> Whatever you have learned or received or heard from me, or seen in me—put it into practice. And the God of peace will be with you. I rejoice greatly in the Lord that at last you have renewed your concern for me. Indeed, you have been concerned, but you had no opportunity to show it. I am not saying this because I am in need, for I have learned to be content whatever the circumstances. I know what it is to be in need, and I know what it is to have plenty. I have learned the secret of being content in any and every situation, whether well fed or hungry, whether living in plenty or in want. I can do everything through him who gives me strength (Philippians 4:9-13).

Together we will look at six steps Paul gives us that will lead us to discover the secret of contentment.

## STEP ONE: CHOOSE OBEDIENCE

When a company takes over another company, there is often a sign displayed that reads "Under New Management." When we invite Christ to take over our lives, we place ourselves under new management, the management of Jesus Christ. He is a benevolent manager. He manages our lives from a heart of love. "The LORD has declared today that you are his people, his own special treasure, just as he promised, and that you must obey all his commands" (Deuteronomy 26:18 NLT).

Under His loving and patient direction, His plan for our lives will emerge as we yield to Him. It is a wonderful plan. It is the best plan, the highest plan designed by the One who created us, knows us best, and loves us most.

The plan is useless, however, unless we make the choice to follow it daily. God will not force us to follow the plan. He is not a dictator, but a loving Father. Moses reveals the desire of His heart in Deuteronomy 30:19: "Today I have given you the choice between life and death, between blessings and curses. I call on heaven and earth to witness the choice you make. Oh, that you would choose life, that you and your descendants might live!" (NLT).

Our choice to obey will guarantee contentment because when we choose obedience we step under the umbrella of His protection, power, and purpose.

A newly licensed pilot was flying his private plane on a cloudy day. He was not very experienced in instrument landing. When the storm worsened, he realized the control tower was going to have to bring him in for a landing. The pilot started thinking about all of the hills and very tall buildings in the area. He began to panic. Over his radio a calm but stern voice commanded, "You just obey instructions. We'll take care of the obstructions."

God sees what we cannot see. He knows what lies ahead. His Word is the instruction manual for life, the road map for the journey, the customized blueprint by which we build and grow. If you want to obey God, you must saturate your life with His Word. That means hearing it, receiving it, learning it, seeing it, and doing it. James urges us to remember that the message God has planted in our hearts "is a message to obey, not just to listen to. If you don't obey, you are only fooling yourself" (James 1:22 NLT).

Obedience gives God permission to work in and through our

lives. Obedience encourages peace in our hearts Obedience brings contentment. Disobedience is the enemy of contentment, because it is sin. When we cherish sin and refuse to relinquish it, contentment is impossible.

Vance Havner, a well-known Bible teacher, said "You cannot break the laws of God—you break yourself against them." We talk a good game, but what is the reality of our spiritual obedience? We talk about prayer, but never pray. We claim that the Bible is God's powerful and life-changing message to us, but never read it. We often criticize others and find fault in their lives because that very same weakness resides in us. We ignore the people in need around us unless there is an audience to applaud our generosity. We sing loudly about our great love for God but nullify His existence in the way we treat our family. It is not enough to know the truth. We are foolish if we really believe that God is impressed with our knowledge of truth. God is pleased by our practice of the truth.

> *We need to search for the handprints of God in the circumstances of our lives.*

Jesus said, "If you love me, you will obey what I command" (John 14:15). Choose to obey. Obedience will bring contentment.

## STEP TWO: UNDERSTAND THAT GOD IS CONSTANTLY AT WORK

There is an important truth in Philippians 4:10 that would be easy for us to miss: "I rejoice greatly in the Lord that at last you have renewed your concern for me. Indeed, you have been concerned, but you had no opportunity to show it." The truth is that God is always at work around us. Sometimes we can see Him working, but many times we can't. Paul's circumstances certainly did not show that God was working. Paul writes, "You have been concerned for me, but had no opportunity to show it." Even though Paul could not see Him, he knew God was working. He believed help was on the way. He stood firm, watching for God. He examined every circumstance, understanding it had already passed through his Father's hands before it reached his life. What contentment to know that anything or anyone who would attack you has to be granted permission by God. Paul was watching and expecting to see His hand at work. And God came through.

We need to search for the handprints of God in the circumstances of our lives. As we search for Him and look for Him, we will become more aware of His presence. There are no accidents with God, only divine appointments made by our heavenly Father. Each one is designed to prove the deep love He has for us. Each one is orchestrated to show His provision for His sheep. That interruption we complain about, that intrusion we resent, may simply be an eternal opportunity sent by Him.

Psalm 32:8 records God's promise to us: "I will guide you along the best pathway for your life. I will advise you and watch over you" (NLT). God is our provider. The word "provider" comes from two Latin words: "pro," which means "before," and "video," which means "to see." In other words, God will see to things beforehand. He is constantly at work arranging the circumstances and ordering our steps so that they will fulfill His perfect plan for our lives.

God caused the church at Philippi to become concerned about Paul's needs. That concern came at the time when Paul needed their love the most. God always comes when we need Him the most. He is the Good Shepherd who meets every need of His dependent and defenseless sheep.

What a precious picture of God's provision we find in John

10:4: "After he has gathered his own flock, he walks ahead of them, and they follow him because they recognize his voice" (NLT). The shepherd is always ahead of his sheep. He is out in front of them. Our Father, our Shepherd, our Provider, is walking in front of us, preparing the way. He has gone before us and will personally lead us through every valley and across every mountain of our lives. He is in every tomorrow, working and preparing those circumstances for us to experience. Even if you cannot see Him, He can surely see you. And when it comes right down to it, I would really prefer that God be able to see me rather than insisting that I see Him.

I love the hope found in 2 Chronicles 16:9: "The LORD searches all the earth for people who have given themselves completely to him. He wants to make them strong" (NCV). It is the hope and expectancy of a child who is watching and waiting, longing to see her Father at any moment. If we learn to live life with this perspective of looking for God in every circumstance, we will find contentment.

## STEP THREE: INVEST YOUR LIFE IN OTHERS

We find joy and contentment when we invest our lives in others. Paul had given his life in service. His greatest joy was to serve Jesus Christ. Before he encountered Christ, Paul had been a teacher and a man of great influence. But the highest title he ever gave himself was "servant." "Paul, a servant of Christ Jesus, called to be an apostle and set apart for the gospel of God" (Romans 1:1). First a servant, and then an apostle set apart for the gospel. The people he served became his family, and in turn, served him by praying for him, encouraging him, and meeting his physical needs.

There was a little boy in the ghetto who believed in God. He was often teased by his friends, who would ask, "If God loves you, why doesn't He take care of you? Why doesn't God tell someone to bring you shoes and a warm coat? Where is the good food you've been asking God for?" The little boy thought for a moment. Then with tears in his eyes he quietly said, "I guess He does tell somebody. But somebody forgets."

Many of us have forgotten that we were saved to serve, not sit and stagnate. Service is not an option for the Christian. It is a command. It is a sacred calling and a source of joy. The most contented people I know are the ones who serve. They have found an outlet for giving. They have discovered their gifts and are using them with joy. It is a paradox in the Christian life that the more we give the more we receive. The importance of being a servant is stressed in Matthew 23:11: "Whoever is your servant is the greatest among you" (NCV).

The terrain of Israel is mostly dry. The few lakes and rivers in the land are major sources of water. The Jordan River is the source of water for the Sea of Galilee and the Dead Sea. The Jordan flows down from Mt. Hermon in a clear and pure stream. The Sea of Galilee is a beautiful place because it has an outlet. It gathers in the riches of the water and then pours them out again to fertilize the Jordan plain. But with the same water the Dead Sea creates total devastation. Because it has no outlet, there is nothing life-giving about the water of the Dead Sea.

When we selfishly hoard the riches given to us by God and become "keepers" instead of "givers," we will become miserable in our self-centeredness. Contentment will surely allude us. The highest purpose in life is to be used by God to impact the lives of others. By the way, He is more concerned about your availability than your ability. You may discover a ministry of visiting people in the hospital, taking care of children, encouraging the lonely, or writing notes of encouragement. If you want to be contented, look for opportunities to give yourself away.

## STEP FOUR: CHOOSE TO PRACTICE THE ATTITUDE OF GRATITUDE

Paul had every human right to be angry with God. After all, Paul had been faithful. He had given up much and endured great pain. And yet the undercurrent theme of this passage is gratitude. It is an attitude chosen by Paul. It is a learned perspective. In this verse, "learned" implies that Paul was educated by experience. In other words, Paul is saying that all of his experiences in life, good and bad, have become his tutor in contentment. "I am not saying this because I am in need, for I have learned to be content whatever the circumstances"( Philippians 4:11).

The word "content" can best be defined as "contained." Don't miss this. Paul had trained himself to focus on his inner resources, the resources his heart contained rather than the outward circumstances of life. He chose to be grateful. He chose to praise God…no matter what. We hear his determination in 1 Thessalonians 5:18: "No matter what happens, always be thankful, for this is God's will for you who belong to Christ Jesus" (NLT).

There is an old poem that captures this idea well.

I rejoice in knowing that
There is no oil without squeezing the olives,
No wine without pressing the grapes,
No fragrance without crushing the flowers
And no real joy without sorrow.

Paul knew he could trust God. He was certain God would come through. Why? God had always come through for Paul.

I love money-back guarantees. We recently bought a car to replace a van with 125,000 miles on it. Our first vacation in the new car was a disaster. We began having trouble the very first day. On our way home, we stopped in four different cities, trying to find a mechanic who could repair the car. No one could explain or find the problem. Needless to say, we were not happy campers. But when we returned home and contacted the dealership, we were told that because of the guarantee on the car, we could get our money back or trade it in for another one. That made me happy.

> *When our hearts are filled with gratitude, we will find contentment.*

Did you know that there is a money-back guarantee on every promise of God? Here it is in Psalm 138:2: "I will give thanks to your name for your unfailing love and faithfulness, because your promises are backed by all the honor of your name" (NLT). Now that is something to be grateful for.

Gratitude not only brings contentment, it brings perseverance and produces strength. God entrusts trials to us, giving us the opportunity to choose gratitude. It is easy to practice gratitude when the seas are calm and the skies are clear. The real test of gratitude is in the midst of the greatest storm of our lives.

Gratitude is wrapped around trust. It contains the element of acceptance. Gratitude understands that God is sovereign and that His ways are not our ways. There will be times when we find it impossible to understand His process, but we can always trust His heart.

In Africa there is a fruit called the "taste berry." When eaten it changes a person's taste buds so that everything tastes good and sweet. Gratitude is the "taste berry" in our spiritual lives. When our hearts are filled with gratitude, we will find contentment. Choose to practice gratitude.

## STEP FIVE: GUARD AGAINST GREED

"I know what it is to be in need, and I know what it is to have plenty. I have learned the secret of being content in any and every situation, whether well fed or hungry, whether living in plenty or in want" (Philippians 4:12). One of the greatest enemies of contentment is greed. A salesman was trying to sell a refrigerator to a housewife. "Lady, you can save enough on your food bill to pay for it." The housewife answered, "We're paying for a car on the bus fare we save. We're paying for a washing machine on the laundry bill we save. We're paying for a television set on the cost of movies we don't see anymore. I don't think that we can afford to save any more money."

First Timothy 6:17 warns us about living a life bent on accumulating material things: "Tell those who are rich in this world not to be proud and not to trust in their money, which will soon be gone. But their trust should be in the living God, who richly gives us all we need for our enjoyment" (NLT). We live in a "stuff"-driven world. It doesn't matter how much we have. It is never enough. The world tells us that the more things we have, the more successful we are. Paul said that his contentment does not depend upon "stuff." He had experienced both wealth and poverty but had learned to find contentment in both circumstances. Paul claimed that his circumstances were his initiation into the truth that real contentment has nothing to do with prosperity or poverty.

We need to understand that greed is not always about material things. We sometimes want other people's gifts, talents, abilities, or resources. We may be driven to have the best and to be the best. We find it difficult to relax and appreciate where we are and what we have. Jesus cautions us in Luke 12:15: "Be careful and guard against all kinds of greed. Life is not measured by how much one owns" (NCV). The wealth our Father wants us to enjoy is far greater than mere money or temporary things. "Keep your lives free from the love of money, and be satisfied with what you have. God has said, 'I will never leave you; I will never forget you' " (Hebrews 13:5 NCV). Now that is a fortune.

How important are your possessions? How do you view them? Howard Hendricks is a great Bible teacher. He and his wife were having dinner with a very wealthy but humble man from a prestigious family. He asked the man, "How did you grow up in such great wealth and not be consumed by materialism?" The man replied, "My parents taught us that everything in our home was either an idol or a tool." What a great perspective. The greatest way to guard against greed is to see our possessions as tools and resources loaned to us by God for us to disperse. Hold them loosely. Invest them in the things that are eternal—people and God's Word.

> Tell them to use their money to do good. They should be rich in good works and should give generously to those in need, always being ready to share with others whatever God has given them. By doing this they will be storing up their treasure as a good foundation for the future so that they may take hold of real life" (1 Timothy 6:18-19 NLT).

I have learned that we cannot outgive God. But when we try, greed will vanish. When we practice kingdom giving, we are making deposits in heaven and taking hold of real life. To discover contentment, guard against greed.

## STEP SIX: COUNT ON GOD'S RESOURCES

Paul's strength and contentment came from a source that was not his own. "I can do everything through him who gives me strength" (Philippians 4:13). Paul invested in a personal relationship, an intimate relationship with Jesus Christ. A personal relationship with Jesus Christ makes all of His resources available to us. Wisdom, guidance, power, peace, love, patience, self-control, and many other godly attributes are all ours through Him. He gives us strength for every area of life. And strength is fertile soil for peace, which brings a harvest of contentment.

"The LORD gives his people strength. The LORD blesses them with peace" (Psalm 29:11 NLT). Paul counted on God's strength and resources—that is why he was contented. I read a story about a man who had to cross a wide river on the ice. He was afraid that the ice might be too thin, so he began to crawl on his hands and knees in great fear of falling through at any moment. Just as he neared the opposite shore, totally exhausted, another man glided past him nonchalantly sitting on a sled loaded with iron weights.

How like us! We crawl through life, settling for our strength and meager resources, afraid that His promises will give way under the weight of our needs. We must understand that there is no limit to His power and no end to His strength. Our weakness is actually the vessel for His strength. Hudson Taylor once noted that "God uses men who are weak and feeble enough to lean on him." God says it this way in 2 Corinthians 12:9: "My power works best in your weakness" (NLT).

Exchange your resources for His. Then you will find contentment.

# 12

# Practicing *the* Circle *of* Encouragement

WE ALL NEED ENCOURAGEMENT. WHEN hard times come and darkness threatens, we need someone to inspire us with hope. But the encouragement we receive is not meant to be hoarded selfishly. God designed encouragement to be given away, dispersed like scattered light in the darkness. When we see someone in need or sense that someone we love is going through a tough time, we must give encouragement.

This is especially vital for those who are struggling with depression. Encouragement is a precious gift that can breathe life into a heart that has lost all hope of ever seeing the light again.

> *God designed encouragement to be given away...*

Second Corinthians 1:3-7 describes the circle of comfort that we can give to others through encouragement:

> Praise be to the God and Father of our Lord Jesus
> Christ, the Father of compassion and the God of all
> comfort, who comforts us in all our troubles, so that
> we can comfort those in any trouble with the comfort
> we ourselves have received from God. For just as the
> sufferings of Christ flow over into our lives, so also
> through Christ our comfort overflows…And our hope
> for you is firm, because we know that just as you share
> in our sufferings, so also you share in our comfort.

Here is how the circle of encouragement works. We all get hurt in life. When we turn to God, He comforts us. We are then able to comfort others. It is a circle of encouragement. We all need to receive encouragement and we all need to give encouragement.

## Step One: Understand What Encouragement Is

There are three different words in the Bible that are translated as "encourage." Each one gives us an important insight into the true meaning of what it means to encourage someone.

### To Encourage Means "to Strengthen"

Isaiah 35:3 tells us to "strengthen the feeble hands, steady the knees that give way." The Hebrew word used here means "to strengthen" or "to grow firm" and contains the idea of supporting someone while they grow strong themselves.

During Hurricane Andrew many people in South Florida had trees uprooted and knocked over by the driving winds and rain. Rather than lose the trees, homeowners would replant them and attach 2x4 wooden braces to their trunks for support while the weak trees grew strong enough to stand on their own again. That is the picture of encouragement. Encouragement can mean to strengthen or support.

## To Encourage Means "to Cheer On"

In 1 Thessalonians 4:18, Paul gives these instructions: "Encourage one another with these words" (NRSV). Godly encouragement is not based on what we are or what we have accomplished, but simply on the fact of whose we are. Hebrews 12:1 tells us we have a "great cloud of witnesses" who stand in the balcony of heaven and cheer us on.

When we give the gift of encouragement, we become "balcony people." Encouragement always has a "you can do it" edge to it. Encouragement is God's love in action. It is the picture of a spiritual cheerleader.

## To Encourage Means "to Be Beside"

First Thessalonians 5:11 tells us to "encourage one another and build each other up." That kind of encouragement demands time, energy, and our availability to the one who needs encouraging. Many times when we are in crisis we do not want someone to say anything or even do anything. We simply need someone to be with us and walk with us through the darkness. If we spell encouragement differently it will be easier to understand. To encourage is to "in-courage" someone, to literally put courage in someone else.

When we put these three definitions of encouragement all together, we can understand what it means to become an encourager. To practice real encouragement is to put courage in someone by strengthening them, by calling them up, and by being with them.

Sandhill cranes are great illustrations of biblical encouragement. These large birds that fly great distances across continents have three remarkable qualities. First, they rotate leadership. No one bird stays out in front all of the time. Second, they choose leaders who can handle turbulence well. Third, all during the time that one bird is leading, the rest of the birds are honking their affirmation. Now that is biblical encouragement! That is encouragement that works.

## STEP TWO: RECOGNIZE WHO NEEDS ENCOURAGEMENT

"Therefore encourage one another and build each other up... and we urge you, brothers, warn those who are idle, encourage the timid, help the weak, be patient with everyone" (1 Thessalonians 5:11,14). This passage of Scripture specifically mentions four groups of people who need encouragement.

### Those Who Are Stuck in Neutral Need Encouragement

Those who are idle tend to be undisciplined. This is someone who is motionless, paralyzed, and unable to move. In other words, they are "stuck" in neutral gear and often do not even want to do the right thing. They need motivation and encouragement to get going again.

Depression can destroy motivation and paralyze even the strongest person. There were days when my greatest accomplishment was to simply put one foot in front of the other. It seemed as if the once-solid foundations of my life had been replaced by murky swamps of bottomless quicksand. I simply could not move ahead—physically, emotionally, mentally, or spiritually. I was stuck and needed someone to pull me out of the mud.

### Those Who Are Afraid Need Encouragement

Timid people are fearful and plagued with doubt. This is someone who knows what to do but is afraid to do it. They want to do the right thing but are bound by fear. They desperately need courage but have none. The key is to get alongside them long enough for them to get past their fear.

Not long ago we bought a ski boat for our family. My daughter was both excited and nervous about skiing. On our first outing on the boat, Danna watched her dad ski and then saw her brother pop up out of the water immediately and ski around the entire lake. I quickly pointed out that the skis and the boat were brand-new, that her dad had been driving a ski boat since childhood, and that if the motor could yank her big brother and dad out of the water, pulling her up would be a cinch. She was really nervous. After several failed attempts, Danna was just about ready to call it quits when Dan turned to her brother and said, "Son, get in the water with her and help her get up." Jered jumped in and began to talk to her, giving her pointers, helping her with her skis, and assuring her that this time she would make it. On the first try, she came up grinning. Dan and I were cheering and hollering every minute of her ride. Today Danna is an excellent skier who cannot believe there was ever a time when she could not ski. When Jered "got alongside" his sister, he lessened her fear by getting under the weight of that fear with her. Then she was able to overcome it. There are times when those who are afraid of the water they are in need us to get in the water with them.

## Those Who Are Weak Need Encouragement

Someone who is weak has no strength and is unable to function alone. All of their strength has been drained from them by some circumstance or series of circumstances in life. They want to do the right thing but are just too weak to get up and do it. They need strength and encouragement.

Depression often leaves you totally zapped of energy. All your resources have been used up just trying to cope with the hole you are in. There are times when you know what you need to do—but you just don't have the strength to get it done.

### Everyone Needs Encouragement

The last phrase of 1 Thessalonians 5:14 says "be patient with everyone." Every person who has ever walked the earth needs encouragement at some point in life. Even Jesus needed encouragement. We all have moments when we are paralyzed emotionally. We all have moments when we are afraid and simply too weak and too tired to keep going. We try to carry those burdens alone while Galatians 6:2 tells us that we need to "carry each other's burdens, and in this way you will fulfill the law of Christ." It is a spiritual reality that we need each other. We were created to share the burdens of each other.

> *We were created to share the burdens of each other.*

I read about a pastor who preached a sermon on bearing each other's burdens. The pastor referred to Matthew 11:29-30 where Jesus tells us to "take my yoke upon you...for my yoke is easy and my burden is light." When he had finished his sermon, one of the church members came up to him and said, "I wish I had known what you were going to preach about. I could have told you something." "Well, my friend," the pastor said, "you can tell me now." The church member asked the pastor, "Do you know why His yoke is light?" The pastor thought a moment and then responded, "Well, because the good Lord helps us to carry it, I suppose." "No, sir," he said, shaking his head. "You see, when I was a boy at home, I used to drive the oxen, and the yoke was never made to balance. Father's yokes were always made heavier on one side than the other. Then we would put a weak ox in alongside a strong bullock. The light end would come on the weak ox and the heavier end on the stronger one. That's why the yoke is easy and the burden is light—because the Lord's yoke is made the same way. The heavy end is upon His shoulder."

Life is filled with burdens that are too heavy for us to carry alone. Jesus came to walk with us, sharing the loads we bear. His strength and love pour encouragement into every step.

> *Sometimes the best encouragement is simply a listening heart.*

In order to experience and be a part of the circle of encouragement, we must understand what encouragement is and realize who needs encouragement.

## STEP THREE: LEARN HOW TO PRACTICE ENCOURAGEMENT

Every day we cross paths with hurting people. A word of encouragement, an act of kindness, a caring smile may be enough to keep them on their feet. We want to be encouragers but may not know where to start.

Here are seven ways you and I can practice encouragement and build each other up in everyday life. These methods are essential for encouraging someone who is depressed.

### Listen to Those Who Are Hurting

"You hear, O LORD, the desire of the afflicted; you encourage them, and you listen to their cry" (Psalm 10:17). Sometimes the best encouragement is simply a listening heart. Listening doesn't require that we fix anything or even that we arrive at a solution.

Listening sends the message "I'm here for you. Just for you. I want to understand and share your pain." We often miss opportunities to give encouragement because we are broadcasting when we should be listening.

I once had an elderly neighbor who loved to talk…a lot. I knew when I ran into her it meant my routine would be interrupted. One day I was out walking when I turned the corner and there she was. I knew I could breeze by her with some lame excuse, but in a rare moment of wisdom, I chose to stop and listen.

I am so glad I did. Her 42-year-old son had just died, and she desperately needed my encouragement.

When we listen to people, we validate their feelings. We invite them into our lives by giving them the most precious gift we have—time. Listening is encouragement.

> *When we listen to people we validate their feelings.*

## Comfort with Your Words

"But my mouth would encourage you; comfort from my lips would bring you relief" (Job 16:5). The spoken word is powerful, and spoken words of encouragement can bring great comfort. The idea is not to speak many words, but the right words. Consider this:

- The Lord's Prayer contains 71 words.
- The Gettysburg Address contains 272 words.
- The Ten Commandments contains 139 words.
- The Declaration of Independence contains 1323 words.
- A U.S. government order setting the price of cabbage contains 26,911 words.

When it comes to words with impact, being long-winded is not a value. But speaking the right words can be life-changing.

Written notes of encouragement often carry even greater impact because they can be kept and read again and again. In the midst of my struggle with depression, I would often slip into a worship service at our church through a side door to escape being noticed. I came in late to worship one day and sat off to the side in order to avoid questioning eyes and concerned stares. My timing was bad because I had managed to get there just in time to welcome the visitors. I simply had no energy or desire to shake hands or smile at anyone, so I sat in my chair hoping everyone would understand and leave me alone. Then I saw him coming. One of our deacons had spotted me and was walking across the auditorium with a big smile on his face. I wanted to run. He put his arm around my shoulder and gently hugged me. He never said a word, but pressed a piece of paper into my hand and left as quickly as he had come. Through tears I read the precious note that said, "I love you and am praying for you. If you or Dan ever need me for anything, I am here." Healing comfort flooded my wounded heart and I found I had the strength to stay.

It's not how long we talk or how many eloquent words we use that matters. It is what we say that is so important. The words we speak are like seeds. What we plant will grow. We can speak words of encouragement that God will take and use to bring hope and give comfort. Comforting with your words is encouragement.

## Get Involved

"May our Lord Jesus Christ himself and God our Father, who loved us and by his grace gave us eternal encouragement and good hope, encourage your hearts and strengthen you in every good deed and word" (2 Thessalonians 2:16-17). When Jered was in second grade, there was a little boy in his class who no one liked because he was a bully and truly obnoxious. One Monday morning this young man came to school with both arms in casts from his shoulders to his wrists. He had fallen out of a tree and broken both arms. The teacher announced to the class that Johnny would need a "volunteer friend" for the next six weeks while he was in the casts. This "friend" would have to help Johnny do everything, from completing class assignments to feeding him lunch—and would even need to accompany him to the restroom.

*What we plant will grow.*

After a few painful moments of silence, one hand went up. I have never been prouder of my son, who volunteered to be Johnny's helper. Jered had struggled to like Johnny, but his sensitive heart could not bear to see the look on Johnny's face when there were no volunteers. I wondered what the next few weeks would hold for my son. As it turned out, I was the one who learned a very important lesson. At the end of the six-week period, three amazing things had happened. First, Jered and Johnny became friends. Second, because Jered was well liked by everyone in the class, the other children decided that if Jered liked Johnny, then they could like him as well. But the greatest change was in Johnny himself. His behavior totally changed. It was as if he decided that since Jered liked him and the other kids liked him, he could be likable.

Sometimes we must become actively involved in someone's life to encourage them.

## Demonstrate Great Patience

"Encourage them with great patience" (2 Timothy 4:2 NCV). Encouragement takes persistence. Persistence takes patience. Just because you have encouraged someone once does not mean that your role of encouragement in their life is over. They did not become discouraged overnight, and they will not often become reencouraged overnight.

> *Encouragement takes persistence.*

Dan first began making wooden furniture a few years ago. My job was to stain and finish the pieces after he had completed them. I had never worked with wood or stain and did not know much about how to accomplish the task. But I knew who did. I headed to our local hardware store. I explained to a salesclerk that I wanted to finish some furniture—today. I was in a hurry to place it in just the right spot in the house and wanted to get this staining business over with quickly. He smiled and patiently explained that it takes time to achieve the best finish. He obviously did not understand my timetable, so I tried to explain again. Ignoring my words, he said that a beautiful finish requires repeated layers of stain and lacquer with time to dry in between. There are no shortcuts if you want the final product to be right.

Encouragement is like that. It takes layers of love and great patience to replenish, restore, and put courage back into a heart. Patience is an important part of encouragement.

## Offer Sensitive Instruction

Second Timothy 4:2 also says that we are to encourage others with careful instruction, being sensitive to the condition of the learner, to the one who is in need of encouragement. Learning does not begin with the truth. Learning begins with the learner and requires loving flexibility.

> *Instruction that is wrapped with*
> *encouragement really works.*

When Danna first played softball, her coaches were her dad and Garland Robertson, our youth pastor. Jered was an assistant coach. At one of their practices, one girl was having trouble hitting the ball. Garland was pitching—and that may have been the problem. Dan was giving her instructions—and that may have been the problem. For whatever reason, she was not hitting the ball. Finally, Jered pulled her aside and worked with her for 30 minutes. He was gentle and gave suggestions with great sensitivity. All of a sudden, the girl who was missing every pitch hit five in a row.

Instruction that is wrapped with encouragement really works. No one cares how much you know until they know just how much you care. I have heard it said that advice and instruction are like snow. The softer they fall—the deeper they stick. Sensitive instruction is encouragement.

### Stay Close

It is encouraging to know that we are not alone, that someone else is close by, in the rocking boat with us. Remember that one of the definitions of encouragement is "to be beside." Sometimes the best way to encourage someone is to stay close by. Join them in what they are doing. A shared joy is a double joy, but a shared sorrow is half a sorrow. God has given us to each other so that we can share the load. A shared load is always a lighter load. Ecclesiastes 4:12 gives us a wonderful promise: "Though one may be overpowered, two can defend themselves. A cord of three strands is not quickly broken."

I read about an ingenious teenager who grew tired of reading bedtime stories to his little sister. So he decided to record several of her favorite stories on tape. He gave her a tape player and plugged in the tape. "Now you can hear your stories anytime you want. Isn't that great?" he said. She looked at the machine for a moment and then replied, "No. It hasn't got a lap."

> *Encouragers look for opportunities to work.*

We all need a lap. We all need the closeness of relationship. We all need to know we are loved. We all need encouragement. Together we will find the encouragement that we need. Staying close to those who need you brings them encouragement.

### Practice Encouragement Daily

"Encourage one another daily" (Hebrews 3:13). An encourager is one who knows you as you are, understands where you've been, accepts who you've become, and still gently invites you to grow. How often do we need to practice encouragement?

Daily. Continually. Constantly.

The key to constant and daily encouragement is to vary our forms of encouragement and whom we encourage. Encouragers look for opportunities to work. Acts 4:36 tells us about a man who came to Christ and his life was changed so dramatically that he sold his land and brought the money to give to God through the early church. That is very impressive. But the most impressive thing about this man called Joseph is that the disciples changed his name. They called him Barnabas, which means "Son of Encouragement."

Are you an encourager? Would your friends suggest changing your name? Would your spouse or your children? What about your neighbors or that person in your life who is struggling to find a ray of light in their darkness?

The message is clear. Just as Christ has come into our lives to encourage us, we are to give that encouragement away. The most amazing truth is that the more encouragement we give, the more we will receive in the circle of encouragement.

Jesus promises, "If you give, you will receive. Your gift will return to you in full measure, pressed down, shaken together to make room for more, and running over. Whatever measure you use in giving—large or small—it will be used to measure what is given back to you" (Luke 6:38 NLT).

## A FINAL THOUGHT

When Danna was a little girl, one of her favorite things to do was to color in one particular art book. It had several pages that were special. I remember one in particular that had a picture of a butterfly. When I looked at it, I couldn't understand her excitement because it was a dull gray. When I asked her why she liked it so much, she said, "Watch, Mommy." She rubbed her little hands together until they were warm and then laid her hand on the butterfly. The warm touch of her hand caused the special inks in the picture to react and the dull gray was transformed into a stunning rainbow of color.

This cold and dark world is hungry for the touch of someone who cares, for a word of kindness, for an act of compassion. This world—your world—is reaching out to you for encouragement.

Let's be encouragers.

# 13

# Embracing *a* Life *of* Balance

As I watched the movie *Twister*, I was reminded of the small Texas town in which I grew up. Tornadoes were a common occurrence in Brownwood. In fact, we would often have "tornado drills" in order to prepare for the next storm. When ominous dark clouds began gathering and the possibility of tornadoes increased, warning sirens would scream through our quiet little town, sending every man, woman, and child scurrying for safety. My family's safe place was an old musty storm cellar in the backyard where we huddled until the "all clear" siren sounded. Breathing a sigh of relief, we then climbed out of that dark cellar to resume normal life.

At times it seems as if a twister has just landed in the middle of my world. Chaos reigns, spinning emotions out of control. Frustration, confusion, stress, exhaustion, and darkness are all too familiar companions. During turbulent times, my first reaction is often to run away and just hide until the storm passes over. But I have come to realize that there will always be another storm, and what I *must* do is learn how to prepare for the storm *before* it hits. Failure to prepare for a storm will eventually result in devastation and ruin. And so it is with life.

When we struggle to set boundaries, failing to establish margins of time for the unplanned and unexpected, we unwittingly surrender to living an empty life of simply "doing the next thing." The result is a harmful imbalance.

Depression prospers in an unbalanced life, thriving in the vacuum of clear purpose and sure direction. The pit of darkness is a common destination for those who refuse to measure and balance the sometimes overwhelming demands of home, career, family, friends, and personal growth. The result is often a frenzied and confusing darkness that will remain until a holy balance is firmly entrenched in its place. It is a balance that only God can bring.

In the Gospels of Luke and John, we find the familiar story of two women, Mary and Martha. They are women just like you and me, and their lives offer a profoundly simple but practical three-step plan for living a balanced life from which we can garner strength for every storm and find light even in our darkest moments.

> Now as they went on their way, he [Jesus] entered a certain village, where a woman named Martha welcomed him into her home. She had a sister named Mary, who sat at the Lord's feet and listened to what he was saying. But Martha was distracted by her many tasks; so she came to him and asked, "Lord, do you not care that my sister has left me to do all the work by myself? Tell her then to help me." But the Lord answered her, "Martha, Martha, you are worried and distracted by many things; there is need of only one thing. Mary has chosen the better part, which will not be taken away from her" (Luke 10:38-42 NRSV).

Then, six days before the Passover, Jesus came to Bethany, where Lazarus was who had been dead, whom He had raised from the dead. There they made Him a supper; and Martha served, but Lazarus was one of those who sat at the table with Him. Then Mary took a pound of very costly oil of spikenard, anointed the feet of Jesus, and wiped His feet with her hair. And the house was filled with the fragrance of the oil (John 12:1-3 NKJV).

Now, I have to admit that Martha is a girl after my own heart! I imagine her as a perfectionist and recognized by all who knew her to be disciplined, strong-willed, energetic, and practical. Martha shared a home with her sister, Mary, and their brother, Lazarus. They were a close family, living in a small town named Bethany, which was located two miles from Jerusalem. From the glimpse we have of Martha from the Scriptures, it's easy to picture her as a wonderful cook and homemaker. In fact, she might well have been considered the "Betty Crocker" of Bethany. Jesus and His disciples knew they always had an open invitation to this home. Martha seemed to be an intense woman with deep feelings and sure convictions, but she certainly had faults just as we do. I rather think that, at times, she may have missed some of the higher moments of life because she was "too busy." Sound familiar?

Now Mary, Martha's sister, is an entirely different story. I believe she must have lived for the higher moments in life. A free spirit and strong individualist, Mary probably saw little value in trivial nuisances such as material wealth, a clean house, cooked meals, and strict schedules. For Mary, nothing compared to the cherished treasures of quiet, peace, truth, and freedom. I suspect Mary was an avid learner who thrived on anything that compelled her to think and reflect. Mary was almost childlike in her hunger for truth—especially spiritual truth—and like her sister, felt things deeply. Sometimes those feelings drove her to do things others could not understand. For example, in Jesus' time it was unusual for a woman to sit among men. But Mary did. She sat at Jesus' feet while He taught His disciples. She was brave. To go against the "norm," daring to be different and perhaps even living in the shadow of her very successful and highly regarded sister, must have taken courage. Yet Mary was also human and imperfect. To some, she may have seemed lazy and flighty or even a procrastinator.

Mary is often considered the spiritual sister while Martha is thought to be not so spiritual. We tend to look at their lives and say we should endeavor to be like Mary. However, I want us to recognize that the lives of *both* women offer invaluable life lessons and truths about balance. A life that is balanced by the power, presence, and purpose of God will not easily fall prey to the darkness of depression. In other words, if we want to get out of the pit—and stay out of the pit—we must embrace a life of balance. God is not the author of confusion, nor does He create chaos, setting His children up to drown in the raging seas of darkness, burnout, and exhaustion. We do a great job of that all on our own. But we can learn important lessons from Mary and Martha, apply them to our lives today, and experience a balance that will bring order and purpose to our crazed world.

## First Truth: We Must Seek God

Balance always requires an honest examination of priorities. Our true priorities are not mere lists of activities completed or goals set, but candid reflections of our heart's desires. The pursuit of God naturally emerges from a heart that longs to know Him. We can say we are seeking God, but the reality is that what we deem important receives the most time, energy, attention, and resources and clearly illustrates our priorities. The importance of right and balanced priorities is first illustrated by the life of Martha in Luke 10:38: "Now as they went on their way, he [Jesus] entered a certain village, where a woman named Martha welcomed him into her home."

Jesus knew He was always welcome in the home of Martha. I'm sure He appreciated the beauty and comfort of this home where He could relax and rest. Martha provided a haven for Jesus. It was a home of replenishment for Him. Scripture tells us Jesus "had no place to lay his head" (Luke 9:58), but He could come to this home when He needed to rest or get away from the demanding crowds. At the age of 30 the Son of God left His natural home, and there is no record of His ever returning to live there. He often went to Bethany, to the house of Martha, Mary, and Lazarus, and even spent His final week on earth there. Obviously Jesus did not have to wonder if He was welcome in this home or if He was an important part of their lives. Jesus knew. He knew without a doubt that this home was His home as well. He did not have to wonder if Martha was ready for His presence. He knew she was always prepared for His presence. Can He say the same about us? Do we have the heart of a seeker, one who lives each day aware of His presence, His plan, and His priorities for us?

Seeking God begins with recognizing who He is and then inviting Him into our lives as Lord and Savior. To make Jesus Lord means that we submit to Him as the boss and ruler of life. If He is not Lord *of* all, then He is not Lord *at* all. He is Holy God, the one who chose us for Himself, the one who loves us and pursues each one of us with a stubborn love that will never give up, the one who created you and me for eternity! On the cross of Calvary, Jesus Christ paid for our sin and made possible a personal relationship with God. Knowing who He is helps us long to know Him intimately. And the more we know Him, the easier it is to understand that a balanced life is one where He is fully in charge, gently leading with the heart of a benevolent Father who desires the highest and best for His child.

Some of us have taken that first step, inviting Jesus to take control, and yet before we know it we find ourselves once again at the center of chaos and confusion. Our problem is not that we lack a personal relationship with God. Our problem is we are not making room for that relationship in the light of His lordship, refusing to give up and submit to His complete control. Balance comes when we make room for Him in the everyday moments and ordinary activities of life, yielding to His plan and His will. Many times the problem of imbalance comes as a result of the crowded condition found within our lives. Like the innkeeper, we turn Jesus away at the door of our hearts and minds with the explanation that there simply is no room.

A few summers ago our family vacation led us to Pennsylvania, where we visited the Amish country. I have always been fascinated by these people and thoroughly enjoyed every minute spent in their beautiful and carefully ordered world. As our visit came to an end, I wanted to buy a souvenir to remind myself of the peaceful days we had spent there, but everything I picked up was too expensive. Being a relentless shopper, I was not about to let limited funds stop me! We began to travel up and down small hidden back roads of each community, looking for Amish products known only to a few and those willing to persevere. I was beginning to lose hope when I spotted a small white sign posted on the fence of a quaint and absolutely perfect house. "Amish Crafts," it said. This was it!

My husband and I explained to our young children that this was a very special store and that they must be extremely quiet, hold hands, and not touch anything. I had serious doubts of this actually happening until we climbed out of the car and a sense of peace settled around us like an old familiar blanket. Our voices immediately dropped to a whisper as we tiptoed up the narrow stone path and gently opened the screen door. When we stepped onto the porch filled with beautiful Amish crafts, a woman came out of the house, welcomed us with a beautiful smile, and introduced herself as Mary. She invited us to browse and let her know if we needed any help. I have to admit that I was close to being rude in my pathetic attempts to catch a glimpse of her home through the porch windows. Reading my mind, she graciously offered, "Would you like to come in and look around?" I thought she would never ask!

For the next 30 minutes Mary took us on a tour of her home, giving us a glimpse of a world very different from our own and an uncommonly simplistic lifestyle I desperately longed to experience. The house was sparsely furnished with only the basic necessities, but Mary described her life and daily routine with words such as calm, uncomplicated, peaceful, and serene. When I asked why she had chosen such a lifestyle, she looked me in the eye and sweetly responded with words of wisdom I will never forget. "I have discovered that when my life and my heart become too crowded, there is not enough room for God." Exactly!

An unbalanced life is a life that is too crowded for the presence of God. When we relegate our spirituality to religious activity, we are building a life on the vulnerable foundation of false truths and erroneous expectations. It is just a matter of time until that foundation collapses, plunging us into a sinister pit of darkness and despair. All God really wants is time to celebrate the extraordinary spiritual relationship of Father and child as we pour over His Word and talk with the One who knows us best and loves us most. When the tears fall, He wants to wipe them away, collecting each one so that He can pour them back into our lives as refreshing rains of restoration. God longs for us to forever run into His arms, sharing every hurt and rejoicing in every victory.

The Father yearns to wrap His strong arms around us, bringing the peace we so desperately need. Practicing His presence will naturally produce balance and bring supernatural order to our chaotic lifestyle.

Another important step in seeking God is learning how to determine what is important and what is urgent. Sometimes we don't know the difference, and consequently we have relinquished the control of our lives to unworthy demands dictated by a world that operates in urgent gear. The important never barges in, while the urgent is always an offensive intruder. The important waits patiently, while the urgent demands its own way, creating bedlam and imbalance. Certainly, there are times when the important is also urgent. But we must learn to discern between the two. We wrongly conclude that a busy life is automatically a productive life. We foolishly presume to live as if a full schedule is evidence of a full heart. We proudly wear fatigue and burnout as our spiritual wardrobe.

I have great news for you! You can relax. God loves who you are more than He loves what you do. If you never do another thing in His kingdom, His love for you will not change. He loves you! It is time for us to stop, examine our lives, and resolve to become true seekers of God. Balance is one of the most worthy rewards of seeking God. Balance comes when we deliberately, purposefully set our hearts on the Lord, and choose to nurture what is important instead of settling for the lesser things in life.

## Second Truth: We Must Reset Our Focus

The reality for each one of us is that every moment of every day is focused on someone or something. We either set the focus through which we live and view life or we allow it to be set for us. A balanced life is focused on God as a result of sitting at His feet. What does it mean to "sit at the feet of Jesus"? First of all, we have to stop. Now that is a novel idea for many of us. Mary stopped what she was doing—helping Martha in the kitchen—to come and sit at the feet of Jesus. Of course, Martha immediately began complaining that she had been left to do all of the work while her sister was wasting time. Listen, my friend, there will always be someone who will misunderstand or complain when you choose to do what Jesus told Martha was "the better part" (Luke 10:42).

> But Martha was distracted by her many tasks; so she came to him and asked, "Lord, do you not care that my sister has left me to do all the work by myself? Tell her then to help me." But the Lord answered her, "Martha, Martha, you are worried and distracted by many things; there is need of only one thing. Mary has chosen the better part, which will not be taken away from her" (Luke 10:40-42).

Notice the word "chosen" used in this passage. Mary made a choice, and so must we. Making a choice to sit at the feet of Jesus requires decisive planning, purposeful scheduling, and willful determination. God wants relationship-building time with us every day, which means time at His feet, in His presence, must be our highest priority. It is absolutely amazing to me how I can squander away the best part of my day, leaving Him with the left-overs and scraps of time, and then have the audacity to complain that my life is void of power and purpose. Distractions come from every side. Some of those distractions are good and wonderful things, but they are all still wrong things if they keep us from spending time with God.

Jesus gently rebuked Martha because she had forgotten what was really important. Oswald Chambers writes, "We can choke God's Word with a yawn; we can hinder the time that should be spent with God by remembering we have other things to do. 'I haven't time!' Of course you have time! Take time, strangle some other interests, and make time to realize that the center of power in your life is the Lord Jesus Christ."

Every day you and I choose where we will invest our time. We plan and schedule everything from hair appointments to lunch with friends, but we sometimes fail to schedule the most eternal activity in this life, spending time with God. Do you need the power to live your life above your circumstances? Are you desperate for the peace and balance only He can bring? Do you long for a relationship that will energize you to carry the burdens and passions of this life? Then it is time to take inventory of the demands upon your time and begin sitting at His feet.

Being wrapped up in God's work can easily become a shabby substitute for being wrapped up in His presence. The paradox is that we can only be wrapped up in God's presence when we stop and learn how to wait on Him. While I absolutely hate to wait on anyone or for anything, I am learning that there is a divine purpose and sacred power made available to us in every waiting room of life. Waiting robs me of control. I am forced to face the unknown. Waiting on God may well provide the catalyst that will change my very life course. In each waiting room, He is at work preparing me for the circumstance and the circumstance for me. "Listen to my voice in the morning, LORD. Each morning I bring my requests to you and wait expectantly" (Psalm 5:3 NLT). From those still, quiet moments of waiting and seeking comes a sacred balance that takes root and grows. It is through the choice to wait on God that a seeking heart finds every need met and light in the darkness.

We not only must stop and be still in order to sit at the feet of Jesus, we must learn to listen. Deuteronomy 30:19-20 instructs us with these words: "Now choose life, so that you and your children may live and that you may love the LORD your God, listen to his voice, and hold fast to him. For the LORD is your life." I know that many voices clamor for our attention. The key to a balanced life is to train our hearts toward God and teach our spiritual ears to listen for His voice above all the others.

I taught third grade for several years while Dan attended Southwestern Seminary in Fort Worth, Texas. I was fortunate to be assigned to one of the largest and best elementary schools in town. My class was one of seven third-grade classes in the school, which meant that the first few days of school were always chaotic. The PE teacher was a welcome sight when she appeared at my door to take the students out to the playground. After PE, it was the responsibility of each teacher to pick up her students. Seven teachers trying to get the attention of over 200 students was especially interesting on the first or second day of school when the teachers did not know their students and the students did not know their teachers. However, after only a few days, an amazing thing happened every year. When we lined up to gather our children, it took only a word or two for them to come running. They quickly learned to recognize the voice of their new teacher above all the rest because they listened to her voice all day long in the classroom. We must do the same. In every circumstance and situation, we need to listen for His voice.

Sitting at the feet of Jesus resets our life focus. It is in those moments when we have stopped long enough to hear Him speak that the battle for balance is won. It is after we have been still before Him that we are empowered to embrace a life of balance.

## THIRD TRUTH: WE MUST DISCOVER OUR LIFE PLAN

Both Martha and Mary made their contribution to the Lord. But each did it in her own way, using her own God-given gifts. Together they present a picture of balance for us to emulate. Some of us would love to just serve God, while others are content to only sit at His feet. A balanced life requires both.

A few years ago, I entered and fully expected to win the Reader's Digest Sweepstakes. Danna watched as the mail came each day, bringing yet another card, letter, notification, or promise of great reward soon to come. With each mail delivery Danna grew more excited until she finally asked, "Mom, if you win that twelve million dollars, do you think you might share some of it with the people in our family?" She's good! I considered her request and then told her I could probably be persuaded to part with a portion of my substantial wealth. I could see the excitement dancing in her eyes as she speculated about her portion of the winnings. I had to ask. "Danna, exactly what would you do with that money?" Her reply was quick and certain: "I would buy me a maid so that I will never have to do another chore ever again in my whole life." I hated to burst her bubble. However, it was obvious to me that a dose of reality was called for. I reminded her she had a room to clean and chores to do until that maid did, in fact, show up.

Unfortunately, many of us seem to have a similar perception of God's plan. We keep waiting for a windfall of spiritual resources that will deliver us from any kingdom work or require us to serve in any way. We long for fulfillment and meaning in life but refuse to seek or follow His plan. It is in serving Him within the framework of that "God-created plan" that we will find balance and contentment.

When it comes to kingdom work, the words of the apostle Paul give a clear directive: "Never be lazy in your work, but serve the Lord enthusiastically" (Romans 12:11 NLT). This Scripture is describing the heart attitude we should cultivate as a child of God. It is the attitude of a servant. We are to serve God enthusiastically, with an eager spirit and a pure and holy passion. This kind of service comes when we serve Him with the right gifts and highest motives, and at the right time.

Many of us try to serve the Lord with gifts we or others think we should have instead of taking the time to discover our God-given gifts of service. We see a need, so we must be the one to meet it. A job needs doing, so we jump in to save the world. Because approval and public recognition feed the weakened condition of our spiritual journey, we take on jobs as food for our fragile ego. The result is emptiness, frustration, and waste. Do not squander the precious resources and divine calling of your life by living for the approval of others. Get serious about discovering your gifts and using them to do what He created you to do. The writer of Psalm 139 tells us:

> LORD, You have searched me and known me. You know my sitting down and my rising up; You understand my thought afar off. You comprehend my path and my lying down, and are acquainted with all my ways...For You formed my inward parts; You covered me together in my mother's womb. I praise You, for I am fearfully and wonderfully made; marvelous are your works, and that my soul knows very well. My frame was not hidden from You when I was made in the secret, and skillfully wrought in the lowest parts of the earth. Your eyes saw my substance, being yet unformed. And in Your book they were all written, the days fashioned for me, when as yet there were none of them (Psalm 139:1-3,13-16 NKJV).

Embracing a life of balance requires a personal spiritual inventory in order to discover who we really are in God's eyes. What is the obvious center around which my world revolves? What main message does my life communicate? What is the cry of my heart?

Each one of us is uniquely shaped for service. We were created in response to His plan for our very existence. To determine that shape and experience all that God has for us, we must understand ourselves in a way that only the Holy Spirit can make possible. Built into each one of us are unique gifts, passions, abilities, and talents that resource His purpose and plan for us. Even our personalities, along with every strength and weakness, become part of our individual life plan. Each experience, good or bad, is used by God to shape and mold us into His image. When we understand and live out His purpose, our lives will begin to fall into place and we will experience a peace and balance that can only be found in a life that is centered on obedience to Him.

Remember Martha? We should note that Jesus did not rebuke her for her work, but only for her attitude in her work. We see Martha serving again in John 12:1-2: "Then, six days before the Passover, Jesus came to Bethany, where Lazarus was who had been dead, whom He had raised from the dead. There they made Him a supper; and Martha served" (NKJV). I believe God gave Martha the gift of hospitality so that she could minister to His Son. But what if Martha had said, "I don't want to be Martha! I want to be Mary!" I hate to think of the mind-boggling blessings and rare opportunities we miss giving and receiving in life because we have never truly discovered and used the gifts God has given us. We misuse essential energy and waste invaluable time trying to be someone we were never created to be. As a result, we have no peace, and balance seems to be an impossible dream.

On the other hand, our giving can and should consist of more than gifts of service. "Then Mary took a pound of very costly oil of spikenard, anointed the feet of Jesus, and wiped His feet with her hair. And the house was filled with the fragrance of the oil" (John 12:3 NKJV). Just imagine the heart of Jesus as He watched Mary serve Him with total abandonment, giving Him everything she had. He knew her gift was one of great financial and personal sacrifice. The oil she gave to Jesus cost the equivalent of a year's salary. The house was filled—not only with the fragrance of the oil—but with the sweet aroma of sacrificial service that flowed from a heart filled with right motives.

I am convinced that we do not burn out doing the work of God. I believe that we burn out doing the work of God in the wrong way and for wrong reasons. In other words, we attempt to serve God in our own limited strength. I have learned the hard way that what He calls us to do—He always equips and empowers us to do.

For years I tried to conjure up gifts I did not have and ignored the ones I did have because they were not the ones I wanted or felt I should have. My motives were anything but pure. They were self-centered and wrong. The result was two years spent in a deep, ugly pit of darkness. God used that pit to teach me the unmistakable but freeing truth that when He made me, He included every gift, talent, and passion needed to carry out the life mission He has for me. I began to walk in the knowledge that when I embrace His plan and those gifts, I not only will find joy in serving Him but renewed strength and certain direction as well.

I am told that the Sea of Galilee and the Dead Sea are made of the same clear, cool water that flows down from the heights of Mount Hermon. The Sea of Galilee creates beauty out of this gift because it has an outlet. It gets to give! The Sea of Galilee gathers in its riches and then pours them out again to water the Jordan plain. But the Dead Sea—with the same water—is a place without life. The Dead Sea has no outlet. It only keeps.

When we pour out our lives in God-appointed service, using our God-given gifts, the result will always be restoration and replenishment. The right motives and gifts yield a life filled with beauty, peace, and joy, if we balance those gifts and motives with God's timing. Now I know what you are thinking—it is always the right time to get up and serve God. But the lives of Mary and Martha tell us something quite different.

Balance comes only *after* we have stopped to sit in sweet silence at the feet of Jesus, listening to His voice and absorbing His plan. Then we can't help it—we are compelled to serve Him in response to His love for us and as a result of His power in us. As surely as a fruit tree produces fruit, one who has been at the feet of Jesus will naturally serve Him.

"Abide in Me, and I in you. As the branch cannot bear fruit of itself, unless it abides in the vine, so neither can you, unless you abide in Me. I am the vine, you are the branches; he who abides in Me, and I in him, he bears much fruit, for apart from Me you can do nothing" (John 15:4-5 NASB). To abide in the vine means to rest, to wait for or reside in the strength and nourishment of the vine. Just as a field that has rested and been replenished produces a greater harvest, our lives will be more productive and fruitful when we have tended the soil of our hearts and minds in the right way.

Being out of balance is definitely not a good thing. When the washer is out of balance, it will skip and bump across the floor. When the checkbook is out of balance, we will assuredly hear from the bank. When the tires on the car are out of balance, we are in for a very bumpy ride. When life is out of balance, the results can be disastrous. Priorities become distorted, critical life power is depleted, and the pit of darkness looms just ahead. Coming out of the darkness and staying out of the darkness is achieved as we live each day—passionately seeking God, diligently focusing on His plan, and joyfully serving Him— embracing a life of balance.

# Thoughts *from the* Other Side *of the* Pit

HAVE YOU EVER RECEIVED A gift that you wanted to return but couldn't? I certainly felt that way about the pit of depression. I wanted to take this nasty black hole to the nearest "Pit Store" and exchange it for a tall mountain of victory. But as I now stand on the other side of the pit, I realize I would not exchange this priceless gift for any other. It has become the single most defining experience of my life, and I would willingly go through it again tomorrow for what God has accomplished in my life through the darkness of depression.

## PITS ARE A CERTAINTY

Hard times will come. Darkness will find us. We will at some point in our lives find ourselves in a pit. It may be a pit of wrong choices and foolish decisions we have dug with our own hands. It may be a customized pit prepared for us by the enemy himself.

But a pit is a pit! And all pits are basically the same—dark, lonely, and filled with the ugliness of life.

## PITS HAVE A PURPOSE

Every pit has a purpose. They come to us for a reason. Pits have an amazing way of bringing balance to life: a balance between sorrow and joy, between darkness and light, between faith and doubt, between weakness and strength. Life is like a prescription. The individual ingredients may seem harmful, but when they are blended and balanced, they bring health. Pits are part of the prescription of life.

Pits demand that we change our perspective. They make us stop and scrutinize priorities, eliminating the trivial and focusing on the important. Pits give us new eyes and a heavenly focus.

Pits come to strengthen us. Our struggle to escape the darkness forces us to admit our insufficiency and search for power outside of our own.

## YOU CAN GET OUT OF THE PIT

If there is one central message of this book, it is hope. I made it out of the pit and so can you! The path may seem endless and even cruel at times, but remember that you did not slip into that pit overnight and you will not climb out overnight. The journey out of the pit begins and ends with one small step. Walk straight ahead through your fear. And with each step, moment by moment, the darkness will slowly begin to lift.

## YOU CAN RETURN TO THE PIT

When it comes to pits, there is bad news and good news. The bad news is that those who struggle with depression tend to struggle with it for a lifetime. The good news is that the things that *got* you out of the pit will *keep* you out of the pit. I often step to the edge of that familiar black hole because I want to remember how I got there. Then I throw a party in my soul and rejoice in the journey out!

## YOU CAN LEARN TO STAY OUT OF THE PIT

Hedges of protection must be planted around the pit of depression. Priorities must be set. Balance must be kept. Habits must be cultivated. Accountability must be sought. Lessons must be learned. These hedges must be constantly tended in order to provide constant protection. In other words, keep doing what you know to do.

## GOD WILL USE YOUR PIT

From the depths of every pit comes a message of hope...a message of power...a message of grace. It is a message for us to share. God does not want us to just endure the pits of life. People without Christ can muster up enough courage—enough human strength—to get through a trial, but God has a better plan! He does not want us to just survive the pain. He wants us to rise above it—to celebrate it and use it!

On the other side of the pit you will find that you can minister to others who are in the grip of depression. You understand their fear. You know the reality of their darkness and the depth of their pain. Hurting people will listen to you when they will listen to no one else. Why? Because you were once like them...a pit dweller.

When you begin to share your journey—when you make the choice to help others find their way to the light—God will strengthen you and keep you out of the pit. The choice to use your pit will unleash God's power in your life as never before.

## LIFE IS SWEETER ON THE OTHER SIDE OF THE PIT

We cannot really know just how bright the light is until we

have spent time in the dark. For me, the sun is brighter. The sky is bluer. Every day is filled with the discovery of new little joys. Relationships grow deeper and fuller. Peace settles around me like an old familiar friend. The intimate and faithful presence of a loving Father has become the reality I once dreamed of. And speaking of dreams, there are so many now filling my heart and life!

## A FINAL THOUGHT

A beekeeper once told F.B. Meyer how some of the young bees are nurtured to ensure their healthy development. The queen lays each egg in a six-sided cell, which is filled with enough pollen and honey to nourish the egg until it reaches a certain stage of maturity. The top is then sealed with a capsule of wax.

When the food is gone it is time for the tiny creature to be released. The wax is so hard to penetrate that the bee can make only a very narrow opening. It is so narrow that in the agony of exit the bee rubs off the membrane that encases its wings. When it finally does emerge it is able to fly!

The man telling the story said that one time a moth got into the hive and devoured the wax capsules. As a result the young bees crawled out without any effort or trouble. But they could not fly.

Remember, my friend, it is through the struggle of the trial—the journey out of the pit that the very best part of us takes flight.

Today I am flying! And one day soon you, too, will look around to see that you are coming out of the dark!

# Appendix A:

# Are You Depressed?

FEELING DEPRESSED OCCASIONALLY IS PART of life. But if it lasts more than two weeks, check with your doctor or a Christian counselor. A simple change in diet, medication, or lifestyle may be all that is needed. For many, more extensive help is required.

The following is a checklist to help you determine if you or someone you love is depressed. Are you or is your friend or loved one experiencing:

____ 1. Fatigue or decreased energy

____ 2. Irritability and/or anger

____ 3. Sadness

____ 4. Lack of interest in normal activities

____ 5. Insomnia or oversleeping

____ 6. Weight gain or loss

____ 7. Excessive crying

____ 8. Thoughts of death or suicide

___  9.  Inability to participate in normal relationships

___  10.  Inability to work or carry out normal activities

___  11.  Difficulty in making decisions

Please consider seeking help if you checked three or more items.

## POSSIBLE FACTORS THAT CAN TRIGGER DEPRESSION*

### Physical

- Illness
- Fatigue
- Medication
- Hormonal or chemical imbalance
- Overcommitment of time
- Overcommitment to responsibilities, etc.

### Psychological

- Significant loss (death, divorce, being fired from a job). The natural grief process can turn to depression if it stops in one of its stages.

    Grief process:

    1. Denial

    2. Anger outward

    3. Anger inward

    4. Genuine grief

    5. Resolution

- Rejection
- Major life change

---

\*    These are just *some* of the factors that can cause depression.

- Learned patterns (how you were raised; if you were taught negative thought patterns)
- Midlife crisis (fear of never attaining goals)
- Anxiety
- Growing older (loneliness, loss of mate, no purpose)
- Suppressed anger

## *Spiritual*

- Disobedience
- Aftermath of great victory
- Guilt (false guilt: legalism instead of love and grace; true guilt: conviction of sin or refusal to deal with sin)
- Wrong perspectives
- Wrong priorities
- An unbalanced life
- Perfectionism
- Self-effort (trying to live by own power; empty)
- Self-focus
- Teaching time (dark times may be teaching times)

# Appendix B:

# Promises *for the* Pit!

SOME OF MY FAVORITE VERSES and books follow. I pray they comfort you or someone you love.

> O God, have pity, for I am trusting you! I will hide beneath the shadow of your wings until this storm is past (Psalm 57:1 TLB).

> Because you are my help, I sing in the shadow of your wings. My soul clings to you; your right hand upholds me (Psalm 63:7-8).

> I will lead the blind by ways they have not known, along unfamiliar paths I will guide them; I will turn the darkness into light before them and make the rough places smooth. These are the things I will do; I will not forsake them (Isaiah 42:16).

> Set me free from my prison, that I may praise your name (Psalm 142:7).

> God is our refuge and strength, a tested help in times of trouble (Psalm 46:1 TLB).

He gives power to the tired and worn out, and strength to the weak…But they that wait upon the Lord shall renew their strength. They shall mount up with wings like eagles; they shall run and not be weary; they shall walk and not faint (Isaiah 40:29,31 TLB).

The righteous cry out, and the LORD hears them; he delivers them from all their troubles. The LORD is close to the brokenhearted and saves those who are crushed in spirit (Psalm 34:17-18).

Praise the LORD, O my soul; all my inmost being, praise his holy name. Praise the LORD, O my soul, and forget not all his benefits—who forgives all your sins and heals all your diseases, who redeems your life from the pit and crowns you with love and compassion (Psalm 103:1-4).

Why are you downcast, O my soul? Why so disturbed within me? Put your hope in God, for I will yet praise him, my Savior and my God (Psalm 43:5-6).

I love the LORD, for he heard my voice; he heard my cry for mercy. Because he turned his ear to me, I will call on him as long as I live. The cords of death entangled me, the anguish of the grave came upon me; I was overcome by trouble and sorrow…when I was in great need, he saved me (Psalm 116:3,6).

You have seen me tossing and turning through the night. You have collected all my tears and preserved them in your bottle! You have recorded every one in your book (Psalm 56:8 TLB).

But he said to me, "My grace is sufficient for you, for my power is made perfect in weakness." Therefore I will boast all the more gladly about my weaknesses, so that Christ's power may rest on me. That is why, for Christ's sake, I delight in weaknesses, in insults, in hardships, in persecutions, in difficulties. For when I am weak, then I am strong (2 Corinthians 12:9-10).

"For I know the plans I have for you," declares the LORD, "plans to prosper you and not to harm you, plans to give you hope and a future. Then you will call upon me and come and pray to me, and I will listen to you. You will seek me and find me when you seek me with all your heart" (Jeremiah 29:11-13).

You are my lamp, O LORD; the LORD turns my darkness into light (2 Samuel 22:29).

Then they cried to the LORD in their trouble, and he saved them from their distress. He brought them out of darkness and the deepest gloom and broke away their chains. Let them give thanks to the LORD for his unfailing love and his wonderful deeds for men! (Psalm 107:13-15).

I will give you the treasures of darkness, riches stored in secret places, so that you may know that I am the LORD, the God of Israel, who summons you by name (Isaiah 45:3).

I waited patiently for the LORD; he turned to me and heard my cry. He lifted me out of the slimy pit, out of the mud and mire; he set my feet on a rock and gave me a firm place to stand. He put a new song in my mouth, a hymn of praise to our God. Many will see and fear and put their trust in the LORD (Psalm 40:1-3).

Books that were
especially helpful to me:

- The Bible—especially the book of Psalms

- *Depression* by Don Baker and Emery Nester

- *Reclaiming Surrendered Ground* by Jim
Logan

- *Victory over the Darkness* by Neil T.
Anderson

- *Blow Away the Black Clouds* by Florence
Littauer

- *He Still Moves Stones* by Max Lucado

- Anything written by Barbara Johnson

# What *Am* I Doing *in* This Pit?

KEY VERSES:

*Consider it pure joy, my brothers, whenever you*
*face trials of many kinds, because you know that*
*the testing of your faith develops perseverance*
(JAMES 1:1-2).

KEY TRUTHS:

From the age of ten, our son, Jered, has played football with one goal in mind—to be a starting player on a college football team. When he graduated from high school, and was recruited by a wonderful college that offered him an academic and athletic scholarship, we were ecstatic. Go, God!

Jered was redshirted as a freshman, and during his sophomore year he became the starting fullback. It was so exciting to see our son's childhood dream become a reality. Although his team had a less than stellar season that year, Jered loved playing and had a great year as he developed physically, learned the complicated play system, and took on a veteran mind-set.

The following summer, Jered was unusually excited about the approaching football season. The college hired several coaches who seemed to have a new plan in mind for the upcoming year. All summer long, Jered faithfully ran, lifted weights, watched his diet, and called teammates with the encouragement, "This is our year!" Even the brutal regimen of preseason practice was taken in stride...until the last play of the last practice. I will never forget that phone call from our son. "I hurt my knee in practice today. I have to have surgery, which means I am out for the whole season." I listened in disbelieving silence that quickly escalated its way to fury. Surely, I had heard him wrong. This couldn't be happening because...God wouldn't let it happen, would He? Not to Jered. He had worked so hard. He had been so faithful. Why this? Why now? It's one thing for me to "face trials of many kinds," but it is a totally different matter altogether for my son to face them.

Jered is every mother's dream—sweet-natured, gentle, hard-working—a rare young man of integrity who loves and serves God. How could this "pit" experience possibly be the best plan for his life?

God clearly answered that question for me and my husband, Dan, as we sat in the stands, week after week, watching Jered pace the sidelines on crutches while cheering his team on. He didn't miss a single rehab session, team practice, or team meeting. I never heard him complain or question. Coaches, doctors, trainers, teammates, and parents witnessed a living illustration of the truth that the "testing of your faith develops perseverance." Jered's faith was indeed tested, and he passed with flying colors! He returned the next year as starting fullback, and his team finished the season as the undefeated conference champions. I love it when a plan really does come together!

Are you sitting at the bottom of a pit? Do you feel as if God has not only deserted you but "set you up" for a season of pain and failure? Is your heart filled with anger? Are you discouraged? Celebrate, my friend! God is fully aware of your situation, and He will use it for your good and His glory!

## REFLECTION POINTS:

- Think back to a "pit" experience and remember your initial response. Evaluate that response in light of the truth that since trials develop perseverance, we can face each one with joy.

  _____

  _____

- During that difficult time, did you question God? In what way(s)? Be specific.

  _____

  _____

- Looking back, would you say that the trial strengthened your faith in God or weakened it? Explain your answer.

  _____

  _____

## APPLICATION STEPS:

1. Pinpoint one truth gained from your "pit" experience.

  _____

  _____

2. List specific ways you can apply that truth in your daily walk.

  _____

  _____

3. In regard to this "pit" experience, answer the questions "Why me?" "Why now?" "Why this?"

_____

_____

## MY PRAYER:

Father, forgive me for my complaining and questioning spirit in this pit. Help me to see Your hand at work in every trial and celebrate all You are doing in my life through this difficult circumstance. I choose joy! I choose to believe You and trust You in the darkness as well as in the light. Thank You for the gift of testing and the reward of perseverance. Amen.

## POWER VERSES:

> *Trust in the LORD with all your heart, and lean*
> *not on your own understanding; in all your ways*
> *acknowledge Him, and He shall direct your paths*
> (PROVERBS 3:5-6 NKJV).

# 1

# Understanding Depression

## KEY VERSE:

*I'm eager to encourage you in your faith, but I
also want to be encouraged by yours. In this way,
each of us will be a blessing to the other*
(ROMANS 1:12 NLT).

## KEY TRUTHS:

While I am not a big fan of television, I do enjoy watching
home improvement shows. On a recent program an interior
decorator and home owner were discussing a list of changes that
needed to be made. "First, we have to do something about those
windows," the decorator announced. I was surprised that she had
listed this task first—until I saw the house. The existing glass was
not only an ugly shade of gold, but it was thick and chunky as
well. The windows let in no light and made it virtually impossible to see in or out. The result was a dark, isolated home. The
distressed home owner protested, "But I like my privacy. And if I
thought anyone could see in, I would feel totally exposed."

When it comes to dealing with depression, many people feel the same way. We construct walls over which no one can climb. We fill the windows of our soul with emotional excuses. The result is darkness, loneliness, and missed opportunities for restoration. We don't want to understand depression; we simply want to be rid of it. Many people try to understand and deal with depression on a surface level—refusing to face painful experiences, difficult relationships, and, in general, the broken places where darkness lives. We look for the nearest exit, hoping to bypass transparency because the price is just too high to pay.

Emotional integrity is an essential step to understanding depression. We must be real before we can be right, and until we are willing to risk being transparent, we can neither understand nor deal with depression effectively. Depression is an emotional, mental, physical, and spiritual disorder. Something is out of balance. We have buried pain instead of confronting it. We have misplaced our trust and sought help from impotent sources. In order to deal with depression, we must first come to a place of total and complete surrender to God and His plan of healing—even if we cannot see or do not understand that plan. The bottom line of God's heart for us is always restoration and healing.

## REFLECTION POINTS:

- Are you afraid to drop your emotional guard? If so, why?

_____

_____

- When thinking about transparency, what do you fear most?

_____

_____

- What relationship or circumstance would benefit from your choice to be real?

_____

_____

APPLICATION STEPS:

1. Choose to be emotionally transparent with God and with others.
2. Seek God's plan and determine the first step you need to take toward emotional integrity.
3. Identify, confront, and choose to fight the fear of being transparent.

MY PRAYER:

Father, I admit I don't understand the darkness in my life. I am afraid to face that darkness, but right now, I choose to step through that fear and yield to You and Your perfect plan for my life. I give up my "right" to understand Your processes and choose instead to focus on Your heart of love for me. I praise You now for the light just ahead. Amen.

POWER VERSES:

*Strengthen the weak hands, and make firm the*
*feeble knees. Say to those who are fearful-hearted,*
*"Be strong, do not fear! Behold, your God will*
*come with vengeance, with the recompense of God;*
*He will come and save you"*
(ISAIAH 35:3-4 NKJV).

# 2

# Climbing Out *of the* Pit

KEY VERSE:

*Pride will ruin people, but those who*
*are humble will be honored*
(PROVERBS 29:23 NCV).

KEY TRUTHS:

Tom Brokaw tells this story about humility: He was wandering through Bloomingdale's one day shortly after being promoted to cohost *The Today Show*. He had worked many years in Omaha as well as Washington and Los Angeles. He was feeling good about himself and was enjoying his well-deserved fame when he noticed a man watching him closely. The man kept staring, and then he finally approached him. Brokaw, enjoying his new celebrity status, was prepared to sign an autograph. The man pointed at him and said, "Tom Brokaw, right?" "Right!" said Brokaw. "You used to do the morning news on KMTV in Omaha, right?" Brokaw smiled and said, "That's right!" Tom Brokaw prepared himself to receive the praise he felt he had earned and deserved. "I knew it the minute I spotted you!" the man said. Then he paused and added, "Whatever happened to you?"

Pride and insecurity are simply opposite sides of the same coin. Both are a preoccupation with self and both are destructive elements of depression. In order to climb out of the pit, we must set aside our pride and self-sufficiency, both of which were present in my life while sitting in that pit. I was a pastor's wife, conference speaker, teacher, and musician. I shouldn't have to deal with depression. What would others say if I openly confessed my struggle? After all, a grounded Christian should not have to battle depression—right? While sitting at the bottom of that pit, everything was stripped away. My pain overshadowed my pride while my insecurities slowly succumbed to the grace of God. I realized that He had been waiting for me to get to the place of complete frailty. Then, and only then, was I ready to begin the climb out of the pit.

The Father waits, longing for us to reach the end of ourselves, the end of our useless pride and come to Him just as we are. When we lay it all down and come honestly before Him, I am convinced He pumps His fist in the realms of heaven and shouts, "Yes!" Don't waste another minute trying to navigate the darkness on your own. Your journey out of the pit is just ahead.

REFLECTION POINTS:

1. As you examine your heart, are there any areas in which pride is a factor?

_____

_____

_____

2. If so, why is that pride dangerous?

_____

_____

APPLICATION STEPS:

- Recognize the pride in your heart and soul.
- Understand that pride goes against everything God wants to do in my life.
- Choose to crucify that pride.
- Pray that God will arrange the circumstances of your life that you might know true humility.

MY PRAYER:

Lord, I choose to crucify my pride. I choose humility. (Write your own prayer—in your own honest words—asking Him to give you the opportunity to experience humility. Tell Him your fears and ask Him for strength to walk through them.)

POWER VERSE:

*The reward of humility and the fear*
*of the LORD are riches, honor and life*
(PROVERBS 22:4 NASB).

# 3

# Getting Past Your Past

KEY VERSE:

*He [God] is so rich in kindness that*
*he purchased our freedom through the blood of*
*his Son, and our sins are forgiven*
(EPHESIANS 1:7 NLT).

KEY TRUTHS:

One of the key factors in my battle with depression was dealing with and letting go of past sin and pain. The shadows of yesterday can easily become the dark clouds of today. In order to deal with depression, we must deal with sin—first, in a personal relationship with Christ and then on a daily basis as a believer.

Every believer has two problems when it comes to dealing with sin. First, we must confess it. I know it sounds simple, but many of us have lost our sensitivity to sin because we are aligned with the world instead of with God. The mark of a believer growing in grace is sensitivity to sin. When I was a little girl, I rarely wore shoes. When the first day of summer came along, I would kick off my shoes and store them in my closet—wearing them only when necessary. Even now, I can remember the painful sensations of playing on the gravel road beside our house. The sharp rocks cut and bruised my tender feet—at first—but by summer's end, my feet were rough and calloused. I could run, jump, and play for hours on the rocks that had once caused so much pain.

Sin is much the same. The first time we commit a sin, it breaks our heart, but the next time we commit that same sin, it doesn't seem quite as bad. Our heart becomes calloused to that sin we repeatedly commit and a foothold is formed, making a place for the darkness to reside. We must confess sin completely, confidently, and continually. Jesus is faithful, and He will keep His promise to forgive and to cleanse us from all sin.

> As far as the east is from the west, so far has he removed
> our transgressions from us (Psalm 103:12).

The second problem we have with sin is forgetting forgiven sin. Is that even possible? While we can't totally blot out a memory, we can make sure it's no longer a live issue in our lives. God's way seems too easy. We act as if the Holy Spirit needs our help or as if what Jesus did on the cross was not enough. We feel that we must make additional payments for our sin by *doing* something, when Micah 7:19 is clear about God's attitude toward our sin: "Once again you will have compassion on us. You will trample our sins under your feet and throw them into the depths of the ocean!" (NLT). The problem comes when we revisit confessed sin, when we "go fishing" in the waters of our past.

Sometimes the core of clinical depression is riddled with sin we have never acknowledged or dealt with. Guilt and shame surround each transgression, and because condemnation seems like the logical solution, we allow the darkness to consume us as payment for each sin. An important part of the battle with depression is the deliberate choice to face and deal with sin.

REFLECTION POINTS:

- Ask the Holy Spirit to show you every sin in your life that needs repentance and confession (list each one as it is revealed to you):

- Are you ready to turn away from the sin you have confessed? Explain.

- Do you really believe that God will forgive you? On what basis?

APPLICATION STEPS:

1. Understand that forgiveness requires repentance.
2. Choose to confront and turn from the sin in your life.
3. Be willing to destroy any paths that might lead to that same sin.
4. Trust God for the power to practice repentance and praise Him for the forgiveness He offers.

MY PRAYER:

Father, I am so tired of trying to live today while carrying the baggage of my past. Please give me the courage to face the sins I have tried to bury. Help me to turn away from each one, leaving it in Your hands. Thank You, Lord, for Your grace, Your mercy, and Your love. Please fill my heart with the light of Your forgiveness. Amen.

POWER VERSE:

> *If my people who are called by my name will humble*
> *themselves and pray and seek my face and turn from*
> *their wicked ways, I will hear from heaven and will*
> *forgive their sins and heal their land*
>
> (2 CHRONICLES 7:14 NLT).

# 4

# Discovering *the* Power *of* Forgiveness

KEY VERSE:

> *He has removed our rebellious acts as far*
> *away from us as the east is from the west*
> (PSALM 103:12 NLT).

KEY TRUTHS:

I have discovered that forgiveness releases hurt and chooses to let go of pain. Several years ago a good friend accused me of being a liar. I was stunned! My heart was broken, and even though we talked it through, I could tell she still didn't believe me. For months the sting of her words stayed in my mind and took root in my heart. Darkness seemed to follow me until the day when I cried out to God, laid my wounded heart at His feet, and let go. I forgave her and set myself free! Forgiveness is powerful—especially when battling depression.

In order to forgive ourselves, we must let go of past failure. When I refuse to allow myself to get past my past, it is as if I am gluing myself to my mistakes. Tightly clutching the hurt, I refuse to see myself as more than something I have done—a choice that feeds the darkness of depression. I spent many years trying to earn the approval of God and the applause of man, and authenticate my own sense of value by what I did. The result was disastrous in my life. Nothing I did was quite good enough. I had to be perfect to be acceptable. The pit of depression became my tutor in forgiveness and in living an authentic life.

When it comes to forgiving others, God never says we have to *feel* like forgiving. Honestly, our feelings are irrelevant and untrustworthy. Forgiveness is not a feeling; it is a choice. Forgiveness is an independent act between us and God, totally separate from the response or reaction of the person we are forgiving. We are not responsible for their response. They are! God is! But when we hold on to the hurt, we are refusing to forgive, and that's an attitude that soon becomes a hindrance to God working in their lives as well as in our own. It's time to forgive. It's time to let go of the hurt. Then, freedom from the darkness can come.

REFLECTION POINTS:

- What past hurts still have power in your life today?

  _____

  _____

- Why have you held on to those hurts for so long?

  _____

  _____

- What is the first step you need to take in order to let go and move on?

  _____

  _____

APPLICATION STEPS:

1. Identify the areas in which you have failed to practice forgiveness.

2. Pray through each one, choosing to forgive and let go of the hurt.

3. Thank God for the precious gift of forgiveness that He made possible by His death on the cross.

MY PRAYER:

Lord, I confess to You that I have been hurt and angry about my past. Right now, I choose to forgive each hurt and lay down my wrong attitudes. Will You please forgive me and heal the broken parts of my heart? I trust You to make my life a living illustration of Your forgiving love. Amen.

POWER VERSE:

*He has rescued us from the dominion of darkness and*
*brought us into the kingdom of the Son he loves, in*
*whom we have redemption, the forgiveness of sins*
(COLOSSIANS 1:13-14).

# 5

# Experience *the* Power *of* Right Thinking

KEY VERSE:

> *For the mind set on the flesh is death, but*
> *the mind set on the Spirit is life and peace*
> (ROMANS 8:6 NASB).

KEY TRUTHS:

As I stood on the sideline of the football field where my 18-year-old son was practicing for the South Florida All-Star Football Game, I was *not* prepared for the hideous sounds and horrific sights that assaulted every protective sense I have as a mother. My baby—my 6', 230-pound baby—was knocking padded giants left and right as he bulldozed his way toward the goal line.

Mixed emotions and foreign thoughts skipped through my heart and mind. On the one hand, I was so proud of Jered that I felt like shouting to the college scouts and coaches standing beside me, "That's my boy!" On the other hand, I wanted to drag him off of that field, lock him up in his nice, safe room, and never let him play the barbaric game of football again. The curious thing is that Jered is a gentle young man who loves every animal he sees, will do anything to help anyone in need, rarely gets angry, and is a major hugger! So what happens when he steps on that football field? I'll tell you what happens. He turns into a growling, intimidating predator who bashes heads and bruises any opponent who gets in his way.

On the ride home, I shared my thoughts with him, describing my astonishment at his metamorphosis from the teddy bear I know to the bulldozing bear opponents fear. He laughed and said, "Mom, ninety percent of football is mental. If you *think* tough, you will *be* tough." I could buy that theory, in part, but looking at Jered's size, considerable bulk, and bulging muscles, I had to believe that his physical attributes had something to do with his intimidating bruiser mentality on the field. "Son, you are a hulk. Any player would be afraid of you!" He grinned, loving the compliment, and then he reminded me of a friend who had graduated two years earlier. Chris was a short, lean-but-deadly running back known for intimidating players twice his size. I remembered Chris, as well as Jered coming home from several practices complaining, "I'd rather get hit by anyone on the team than Chris. He is brutal!" My son then said something I will never forget. "Mom, Chris was a great football player because he *thought* he was a great football player. I have seen so many guys who are bigger, stronger, and better players who couldn't begin to play as well as Chris played. In this game, success is not only in the body but in the mind."

What a powerful truth—on the football field and in life. When it comes to dealing with depression, the greatest battlefield for the Christian is the mind. Proverbs 23:7 tells us, "For as he thinks within himself, so he is" (NASB). In other words, what we think about powerfully influences what we will become. Our actions, attitudes, and habits are born in the mind, an off-spring of the thought life we entertain. We can literally change our lives by changing how we think—but we cannot do it alone. God's standard and guideline for the thought life is very clear and demanding. In fact, it's downright impossible!

> Think about the things that are good and worthy of praise. Think about the things that are true and honorable and right and pure and beautiful and respected (Philippians 4:8 NCV).

We choose what we watch and read, the conversations we have, and the time we spend in the Word. If the mind is not filled with good, trust me, the enemy will fill it with bad. The human mind will always set itself on something. Paul challenges us to choose wisely that setting, taking charge of our thoughts by inviting the Holy Spirit to empower God's standard for the mind. If we don't make up our mind, our unmade mind will unmake us. In order to live right we must think right. How about you? Have you made up your mind?

REFLECTION POINTS:

- In the past, how have your thoughts affected your decisions or actions?

  _____

  _____

- How can you control outside sources of influence?

  _____

  _____

- What part can the Word of God play in renewing your mind and dispelling dark thoughts?

  _____

  _____

APPLICATION STEPS:

1. Recognize the power of your thought life.

2. Choose God's worthy standard for your thought life from this day on.

3. When dark thoughts come, confront them with the Word of God.

MY PRAYER:

Lord, I confess to You that my thoughts are not pure. I have allowed the world and outside influences to pollute the mind that should be set on You. Right now, I choose against my old ways of thinking and invite the Holy Spirit to stand guard over my mind. I commit to fill my heart and mind with Your truth. In Jesus' name, I pray and believe. Amen.

POWER VERSE:

*Let heaven fill your thoughts. Do not think only about things down here on earth*
(COLOSSIANS 3:2 NLT).

# 6

# Winning *over* Worry

KEY VERSES:

> *Be anxious for nothing, but in everything by prayer*
> *and supplication with thanksgiving let your requests*
> *be made known to God. And the peace of God,*
> *which surpasses all comprehension, will guard your*
> *hearts and your minds in Christ Jesus*
> (PHILIPPIANS 4:6-7 NASB).

KEY TRUTHS:

Dan has battled high blood pressure since we first married 30 years ago. Hmmm...now that I think about it...there just might be a connection there! Nevertheless, for the last two years, he has struggled with an irregular heart beat, a common condition that drains energy and generally promotes a compelling sense of exhaustion. Dan Southerland is not accustomed to doing anything short of full speed ahead, so you can imagine his frustration and my concern. Little did I know that the opportunity for fear and worry would escalate to a whole new level when, at 2:30 AM on March 15, Dan looked at me and said, "Honey, I think you need to call an ambulance." I already had. Sweat was dripping from his body like rain, followed by waves of excruciating chest pain, dizziness, and nausea. The ambulance arrived six minutes after I called and began to work on my now semi-unconscious husband. I heard one paramedic say, "I can't get a blood pressure reading, pulse or vein." I climbed up on the bed beside my precious husband and in my kindest, most merciful voice said, "Honey, if you die, I will absolutely kill you! You are *not* going anywhere! You are staying right here! Do you understand me?" I then called for reinforcements. "Danna, get in here," I yelled to our 19-year-old daughter, who was already dressed and standing behind me. If her eyes had not been twice their normal size, I would never have known she was terrified. "What's up, Dad?" she asked. That's my girl! The paramedics finally got an IV going and within minutes, Dan was feeling much better.

A quick sidebar: For weeks, I had been telling Dan how much I loved Carrie Underwood's new song, "Jesus, Take the Wheel."

The paramedics lifted Dan onto a stretcher and into the ambulance. Danna said, "Mom, you ride with Dad. I'll follow you so we'll have a car at the hospital." As I climbed into the passenger side of the ambulance, the radio was on, and the first words I heard were, "I can't do this on my own. Jesus, take the wheel!" God's peace settled around my heart and soul like a familiar friend, and I celebrated the love of a God who cares enough about His daughter that He played her favorite song at the precise moment she needed to hear it.

Why do we doubt Him? Why do we worry? Yes, He is Lord of the universe, but He is also Friend of the wounded heart and Shepherd of every valley. He is Love. He is Peace.

Over the next nine days while Dan was in the hospital, God was with me every step of the way, and He will be there for you, my friend. No matter where you are, no matter how hopeless your circumstances may seem, no matter how deep and dark the pit—He is at work in and around you. Just surrender the wheel of your life, trusting Him to make a way.

REFLECTION POINTS:
- Would people who really know you, describe you as a joyful person or a fearful person?

_____

_____

_____

- What is your first reaction to a crisis—worry or faith?

_____

_____

_____

- What habits do you need to eliminate because they are footholds for worry?

_____

_____

APPLICATION STEPS:
1. Memorize one verse of Scripture each week. When you are tempted to worry, quote Scripture instead and worry will vanish.
2. Guard your thought life. Do not watch frightening movies or television shows. Focus on the power and sufficiency of God.
3. Learn to live with a constant attitude of praise. God is in control. Do not trust your own reasoning or emotions. Trust only the fact of God's Word.

MY PRAYER:

Father, I confess the times I have worried instead of trusted. Forgive my lack of faith. I now choose to trust You wholly and follow You completely. Please fill my heart with Your peace as I learn to walk by faith, not by sight. Amen.

POWER VERSE:

> *The LORD says, "I will guide you along*
> *the best pathway for your life. I will advise*
> *you and watch over you"*
> (PSALM 32:8 NLT).

# 7

# Dealing *with* Stress

KEY VERSE:

*Be still, and know that I am God!*
(PSALM 46:10 NRSV).

KEY TRUTHS:

Two years ago my family and I moved from South Florida to Charlotte, North Carolina, a place we have grown to love. The change of seasons, rolling hills, and Southern hospitality have gently drawn us in and made it home. Our house sits on a beautiful lot, our backyard filled with tall trees and a wide variety of birds. Now, I must admit that I have never been a bird-watcher, but I decided that a couple of bird feeders were called for. It was an experiment of sorts. I pictured small, delicately feathered creatures congregating in our backyard to provide beauty and entertainment for our family and friends. Instead, I got large colorless birds that ate huge amounts of seed and grew fatter each day. Pigeons! I got pigeons! They swooped into my birdhouses and pranced in my grass as if to say, "I am here to stay, honey! Better get used to it!" I didn't like their attitude, but what I did find fascinating was their awkward walk. I watched them day in and day out, wondering what God had in mind when He created these comical birds. Details! I needed details! I headed for my computer, determined to solve this small feathered mystery.

According to an article in the *Detroit Free Press,* a pigeon walks the way it does so it can see where it's going. The pigeon can't adjust its focus as it moves. It actually has to bring its head to a complete stop between steps in order to refocus. As a result, the pigeon must walk with its head forward, stop, head back, and stop.

We can learn an important truth from these amusing birds. We need to build into our lives a pattern of "stops" called solitude. Webster defines solitude as "detachment, separation or disconnection." Solitude is when we deliberately separate and detach ourselves from the momentum of our daily schedule in order to refocus and determine where we really are headed. We live in a world that tries desperately to avoid solitude. Yet, it is one of our basic needs and wisest disciplines.

- *Solitude helps us pray:* Early the next morning, Jesus woke and left the house while it was still dark. He went to a place to be alone and pray (Mark 1:35 ICB).

- *Solitude helps us resist sin:* Be angry, and do not sin. Meditate within your heart...and be still (Psalm 4:4 NKJV).

- *Solitude helps us withstand trials:* On my bed I remember you; I think of you through the watches of the night. Because you are my help, I sing in the shadow of your wings (Psalm 63:6-7).

- *Solitude strengthens us:* His delight is in the law of the LORD, and on his law he meditates day and night. He is like a tree planted by streams of water, which yields its fruit in season and whose leaf does not wither. Whatever he does prospers (Psalm 1:2-3).

Most of us tend to think of silence as empty and hollow

instead of full and rich. We fill our lives, homes, and hearts with noise and activity in order to avoid silence at all costs. So much of God is found in the stillness of our heart, soul, and body. All of hell will stand against time spent in solitude because Satan knows the power waiting for us in those tranquil moments, the quiet moments. We must carve out time for solitude and wage battle in order to protect it. The reality is that if we don't come apart, we will come apart. It's time to stop and know Him more.

REFLECTION POINTS:

- Are you afraid of silence? If so, why?

_____

_____

_____

- What is the greatest obstacle to solitude in your life?

_____

_____

_____

- What do you hope to gain from time spent in solitude?

_____

_____


APPLICATION STEPS:

1. Choose to practice solitude today.
2. Select a place to spend time in solitude today.
3. Surrender your agenda to God.
4. Focus on Him and listen for His voice.

MY PRAYER:

Lord, I recognize my need for time alone with You. At Your feet I lay down my schedule, my agenda, and anything else in my life that would keep me from that time. Please give me the power to stop and a heart that longs to hear Your voice. Amen.

POWER VERSE:

> *Be still before the LORD and wait patiently for him*
> (PSALM 37:7).

# 8

# Managing *Your* Emotions

KEY VERSE:

> *A person without self control is as defenseless*
> *as a city with broken down walls*
> (PROVERBS 25:28 NLT).

## KEY TRUTHS:

Have you learned the truth that your emotions are unreliable? For years I kept hoping that I would one day get to the place where I could count on my emotions for guidance and direction. I have concluded that it's not going to happen this side of heaven. That's the bad news. The great news is that we don't have to rely upon emotions that seem to change like the wind. Instead, we can firmly rely upon the fact that God's truth never changes.

Not only are emotions unreliable, they can take us down with them. That's the picture the key verse in Proverbs is painting for us. When there is no control of self, when there is no grace erecting a hedge of protection around us, we are sitting ducks and vulnerable to attacks from every direction and every enemy.

The key to managing emotions is peace. Peace is a Person. Paul tells us in Ephesians 2:14 that "Christ himself is our peace" (NCV). True peace has nothing to do with human beings, human effort, or human circumstances. True peace cannot be produced on a human level at all. Any emotion we work up and name "peace" is fragile and unable to stand firm in the battle of everyday life. Peace is the result of God's presence and power at home within us.

> Therefore, since we have been made right in God's sight by faith, we have peace with God because of what Jesus Christ our Lord has done for us (Romans 5:1-2 NLT).

Peace is the condition of wholeness and the sense of well-being that comes from knowing God. Peace is dependent upon God's presence in us. We come into this world with an ache in our soul, a longing in our heart, and a deep sense of being lost, but when we find God, we find home where peace takes up residence. Then, and only then, can our emotions be harnessed and used for good.

REFLECTION POINTS:

- What emotion is stampeding out of control in your life?

  _____

  _____

  _____

- What have you done in an effort to control that emotion? What has been the result?

  _____

  _____

  _____

- What new choice do you need to make in order to bring that emotion under control?

_____

_____

APPLICATION STEPS:

1. Read and memorize Proverbs 23:12. How does this truth apply to controlling emotions?

_____

_____

2. Identify and eliminate the sources of fear and worry in your life. Surrender each one to the power and control of the Holy Spirit.

3. When an emotion is overwhelming, stop, take a deep breath, and focus on God. Memorize the following verses and speak them out loud when you are tempted to lose control:

> Proverbs 3:7
> Isaiah 17:7
> Mark 8:34-35
> Hebrews 13:5

MY PRAYER:

Father, I surrender the control of my emotions to You. I can't control them on my own. I don't want to live in emotional chaos. Thank You for the power of Your Holy Spirit. Amen.

POWER VERSE:

> *A fool vents all his feelings, but a*
> *wise man holds them back*
> (PROVERBS 29:11 NKJV).

9

# Getting Good *at* Being You

**KEY VERSE:**

*Before I made you in your mother's*
*womb, I chose you*
(JEREMIAH 1:5 NCV).

**KEY TRUTHS:**

Beginnings are very important. In fact, the place of origin has much to do with the quality of the journey as well as the final destination. My journey—like yours—began in the heart and mind of God. Before I took even one breath, God loved and planned me. That same truth applies to you, my friend. You are no accident! You and I were created in response to the love of God.

> I praise you because you made me in an amazing and wonderful way. What you have done is wonderful. I know this very well. You saw my bones being formed as I took shape in my mother's body. When I was put together there, you saw my body as it was formed. All the days planned for me were written in your book before I was one day old (Psalm 139:14-16 NCV).

God Himself supervised our formation. We were created—not to be a puppet—but for an intimate relationship with God. When Jered was four years old, we enrolled him in a daycare two days a week. Jered loved to play with other children and always got along with everyone. I was surprised when his teacher asked me to come in for a conference. "Jered is a wonderful little boy," she began, "but there is one problem. How long has he known he was adopted?" I was still clueless but answered, "Since he began talking. We have told him repeatedly how special he is and that he is a chosen baby." She smiled and went on to explain that Jered told the other children that he was special because he was adopted. In fact, Jered informed each child that his mom and dad had chosen him while their parents "got stuck" with them.

Listen, my friend, when you begin to understand and live out the eternal truth that you are loved, planned, wanted, and chosen by God, His plan and purpose will naturally unfold before you each day. Remember, in His eyes you are special!

## REFLECTION POINTS:

- Do you really believe God loves you unconditionally?

_____

_____

- What proof of that belief is evident in your life?

_____

_____

- Do you consider yourself worthy? Why or why not?

_____

_____

APPLICATION STEPS:

Read Psalm 139 each day for one month. Record new truths you learn, changes in your perspective, and any fresh insights for your life journey. At the end of the month, write Psalm 139 in your own words and share it with a friend.

MY PRAYER:

Father, I want to know You and find Your plan for my life. I choose to see myself through Your eyes and praise You for Your love. Help me to walk each day in the knowledge that I am Your child. Amen.

POWER VERSE:

*"I know what I am planning for you," says the*
*LORD. "I have good plans for you, not plans to hurt*
*you. I will give you hope and a good future"*
(JEREMIAH 29:11 NCV).

# 10

# Making Friends

KEY VERSE:

*Though one may be overpowered,*
*two can defend themselves A cord of*
*three strands is not quickly broken*
(ECCLESIASTES 4:12).

KEY TRUTHS:

I was raised to be independent and strong. That independence was tested the day my fifth grade teacher announced the upcoming spring festival, reminding us to choose our partner for the three-legged race. I thought little about it until my leg was stuffed in a potato sack with Sandra Long. The girl was totally clumsy and refused to follow my directions. We lost miserably. Why? We were both convinced we could do it on our own. The truth that we were created to need each other is never more evident than when we are battling depression.

One of the main factors leading to clinical depression in my life was the absence of replenishing friendships. As I think back to that time, I am sure many women would have counted themselves as my friend when, in reality, they were simply acquaintances—because that was all I would allow them to be. My pride kept me from admitting that I wasn't Superwoman, that I was fallible and not sufficient unto myself. I refused to take the risk of being hurt, rejected, or misunderstood. I didn't have time to invest in building intimate friendships and was too busy doing the work of God to be a friend. As a result, when the darkness hit, I felt isolated and alone.

Friendship took on an entirely different meaning in my life from that point on. In fact, friends are a great source of strength and encouragement in my life today. Friends fast and pray for me, holding me accountable and confronting me when they see my priorities askew. Friends make me stop and take time for fun. Friends have taught me to be transparent. Have I been hurt along the way? Yes. Have I been misunderstood? Yes. Have the friendships been worth the price? Absolutely! The more I give myself away in friendship, the more love and encouragement I find in friends.

## REFLECTION POINTS:

• What is the greatest hindrance to friendship in your life?

_____

_____

_____

• What has been the greatest reward of friendship in your life?

_____

_____

_____

• Are you willing to take the risk of cultivating intimate friendships and of being a true friend?

_____

_____

_____

APPLICATION STEPS:

Make a list of your two best friends and then picture life without them. What would that picture look like?

_____

_____

_____

Evaluate yourself as a friend. Make a list of friendship goals. You may want to begin with these:

• I will not criticize my friends to other people.
• I will cheer the successes of my friends.
• I will encourage my friends in their strengths and never use their weaknesses against them.
• I choose to love my friends as is!

MY PRAYER:

Father, You are the greatest friend I have. Thank You for creating me in such a way that I need others. Forgive my arrogance and pride in thinking that I need no one. Open my eyes to the people around me and teach me how to be a friend. Amen.

POWER VERSE:

*Do not let any unwholesome talk come out of your mouths, but only what is helpful for building others up according to their needs*
(EPHESIANS 4:29).

## 11

# Learning *the* Secret *of* Contentment

**KEY VERSES:**

*I have learned to be content whatever the circumstances. I know what it is to be in need, and I know what it is to have plenty. I have learned the secret of being content in any and every situation, whether well fed or hungry, whether living in plenty or in want. I can do everything through him who gives me strength*
(PHILIPPIANS 4:11-13).

**KEY TRUTHS:**

For much of my life, I kept waiting for "it" to happen. I had convinced myself that everything would be better after I got married and had a family. Sound familiar? We tell ourselves that life will be complete when our spouse gets his or her act together, when we get a nicer car, when we get that promotion, when we are able to go on our dream vacation, or when we retire.

The pit of depression is filled with an echoing chorus of "what if." Hopes turn to despair and unrealized dreams fill our thoughts.

We have forgotten a very important truth—God is always at work around us. Sometimes we can see Him working, but many times we can't. Contentment is based on trust, and trust is based on acceptance. When we learn to accept and embrace life—the good and the bad—we will experience contentment.

Life will always be filled with challenges, dark times, and trials. We live in a broken world, but because God lives, we can experience joy and contentment.

*Stop waiting…*

*…until your car or home is paid off*
*…until you get a new car or home*
*…until your kids leave the house*
*…until you go back to school*
*…until you finish school*
*…until you lose 10 lbs.*
*…until you gain 10 lbs.*
*…until you get married*
*…until you have kids*
*…until you retire*
*…until summer*
*…until spring*
*…until winter*
*…until fall*
*…until you die*
*There is no better time than right now to be happy.*
*Happiness is a journey, not a destination.*
*Work like you don't need money.*
*Love like you've never been hurt.*
*And dance like no one's watching.*

AUTHOR UNKNOWN

REFLECTION POINTS:

- Would the people in your life describe you as contented?

  _____

  _____

  _____

- Why? Why not?

  _____

  _____

  _____

- What step do you need to take in order to experience contentment?

  _____

  _____

  _____

APPLICATION STEPS:

1. Identify areas of discontentment in your life. Surrender each area to God, choosing His peace instead.
2. Recognize that God's plan for your life will bring contentment and choose now to follow that plan. Write out this new commitment and keep it in your Bible. Refer to it often.

MY PRAYER:

Father, forgive me for not trusting You. Help me to keep my glance on my circumstances and my gaze on You. Today, I choose joy and contentment. I choose to trust You even when I don't understand Your process. I know I can trust Your heart of love for me. Amen.

POWER VERSES:

> *He who dwells in the secret place of the Most*
> *High shall abide under the shadow of the Almighty.*
> *I will say of the LORD, "He is my refuge and my*
> *fortress; My God, in Him I will trust"*
> (PSALM 91:1-2 NKJV).

# 12

# Practicing *the* Circle *of* Encouragement

KEY VERSES:

*Encourage one another and build*
*each other up...And we urge you, brothers,*
*warn those who are idle, encourage the timid, help*
*the weak, be patient with everyone*
(1 THESSALONIANS 5:11,14).

KEY TRUTHS:

We all need encouragement, especially during the tough times. As I battled depression, I was amazed at the people God sent to encourage me. Phone calls came from friends we hadn't seen in years. "I don't know what is going on in your life, but I have had you on my heart," they would say. Notes and letters arrived in the mail—all filled with encouraging words. One of the most precious groups of encouragers was comprised of the elders at our church. Dan would tell them which service I was attending and they would plan their strategy. Our auditorium had three main aisles. An elder would walk those aisles before and after the service, keeping an eye on me. If they sensed I was in trouble or caught in a draining conversation, they would take me by the arm and say, "Excuse us, please. Mary is needed elsewhere." I was then ushered to my car, hugged, and told, "We are praying for you. Go home." It was amazing! It was also a main factor in my recovery. The reason these special men offered me encouragement was because I openly and honestly shared my pain. Doing so invited them into my life. Now that I am on the other side of that pit, I remember the love and encouragement they gave me—and I am motivated to encourage others in God's circle of encouragement.

REFLECTION POINTS:

• Do you really believe that if you ask God for help and encouragement, He will bring it?

_____

_____

_____

• How does the encouragement of others impact your life?

_____

_____

_____

• Who in your life needs your encouragement?

_____

_____

_____

APPLICATION STEPS:

1. If you need encouragement, think of two people with whom you can share that need and make a plan to do so.

2. Look for people in your life to encourage.

3. Either in your journal or below, record the times when you
   have received and given encouragement and the results.

   _____

   _____

   _____

MY PRAYER:

Father, I admit that the thought of being transparent enough
to ask for help is frightening. Give me the courage to be honest
with myself and with others. Give me eyes to see those You bring
into my life who need my encouragement. Thank You. Amen.

POWER VERSE:

*Let us think about each other and help*
*each other to show love and do good deeds*
(HEBREWS 10:24 NCV).

# 13

# Embracing *a* Life *of* Balance

**KEY VERSES:**

> *Abide in Me, and I in you. As the branch cannot*
> *bear fruit of itself, unless it abides in the vine, so*
> *neither can you unless you abide in Me.*
> *I am the vine, you are the branches; he who abides*
> *in Me and I in him, he bears much fruit, for apart*
> *from Me you can do nothing*
> (JOHN 15:4-5 NASB).

**KEY TRUTHS:**

For years I tried to earn the love and approval of God by doing everything I could find to do in ministry. If a position needed filling, I filled it. If a job needed doing, I did it. If volunteers were called for, mine was the first hand raised. After all, if I was doing all of these important things, then I must be important too. Right? The result was two dark years spent at the bottom of a deep, ugly pit called clinical depression. It was as if God allowed me to run to the end of myself, and then He shut the door and turned out the lights. I heard Him loud and clear. "That is enough! It is time for you to abide in Me." I knew very little about "abiding" but a whole lot about "doing."

One of the main factors in my depression was that I didn't understand how to live a balanced life. I found it difficult to set boundaries, failed to establish margins of time for the unplanned or unexpected, and unwittingly surrendered my God-ordained priorities to the empty, vain addiction of just "doing the next thing." Balance can easily become a casualty of this ongoing battle. While sitting in the darkness, waiting on God, I discovered that the pit of despair is a common destination for those who refuse to measure and balance the sometimes overwhelming demands of home, family, friends, work, and personal growth. I had been running the race for the wrong audience and, as a result, relied on my own power instead of God's power.

I wish I could tell you that I now lead a perfectly balanced life, but the truth is that I constantly have to reevaluate my priorities and goals in order to find the holy balance God intends. I constantly have to make difficult choices between the good things and the best things. When I make the wrong choices, I can sense myself sliding toward the dangerous edge of darkness. I don't want to go there again—so the battle continues. The good news is that I don't have to fight alone. God is with me, urging me toward the light and His restorative power.

REFLECTION POINT:

- Is your life out of balance in any area? If so, what are the areas you need to bring under God's control?

_____

_____

_____

APPLICATION STEPS:

Take a day this week for a silent retreat. Go to the beach—a park—your back yard. Just get alone with God and take a spiritual inventory of your priorities, time management, and goals. The results may surprise you.

MY PRAYER:

Father, I desperately need Your guidance in setting the priorities and goals in my life. I want to please You and do what You have created me to do. Help me to see and do Your plan. Amen.

POWER VERSE:

*Listen to my voice in the morning, LORD.*
*Each morning I bring my requests to*
*you and wait expectantly*
(PSALM 5:3 NLT).

# Thoughts *from the* Other Side *of the* Pit

**KEY VERSE:**

*If you love me, you will do the things I command*
(JOHN 14:15 ICB).

**KEY TRUTHS:**

I pray that the study of this book has been a source of encouragement, fresh insight, and new perspective. Now comes the most important and most difficult part—applying the truth God has given. Every time we read or hear the Word of God, we have a choice to make. We can either file it away or put it into practice. God is not nearly as interested in how much we know as He is in how much we do. John tells us that if we truly love God, we will obey Him and do the things He has commanded us to do.

If you are battling depression, I know it seems like an impossible mountain to climb. In fact, it is impossible—on your own. Now is the time to give up! Stop trying to fix yourself and yield instead to the power of the Holy Spirit at work in your life. The battle really does belong to the Lord. God has the answer for every question you have asked. He has the plan for every step of your journey out of the pit. All He asks is that you stop and let Him carry you. He will direct every step and bring the resources and people into your life as part of His orchestrated plan of restoration. Trust God! His heart is for you.

God is neither angry with you nor surprised at your circumstances. You may not understand what He is doing, but you can trust Him to do what is best for you. Set aside your own plans and yield to His. Stop relying on your own strength and lean on Him. And know this, my friend! God is at work in and around you. God has gone before you to order each step and monitor every storm. Rest assured that He is Lord of every mountain, Shepherd of every valley, Friend of every wounded heart...and He adores you! Lift up your head! The best is just ahead!

REFLECTION POINT:

What has been the most life-changing truth you have learned in this study?

---

---

---

APPLICATION STEPS:

Record spiritual markers, life changes, course corrections, or new "light" you have received through the study of *Hope in the Midst of Depression* in a "Victory Journal."

MY PRAYER:

Father, thank You for who You are and who You want to be in my life. I praise You for the changes You have made through the study of Your Word. I choose to obey You, Father. And when

I fail, I celebrate Your eternal forgiveness. Empower me for Your service. Deliver me from the pit of darkness so that I may tell others where they can find Light. I promise to give You all the glory and honor. Amen.

POWER VERSES:

*I pray that from his glorious, unlimited resources*
*he will give you mighty inner strength through his*
*Holy Spirit. And I pray that Christ will be more and*
*more at home in your hearts as you trust in him.*
*May your roots go down deep into the soil of God's*
*marvelous love. And may you have the power to*
*understand, as all God's people should, how wide,*
*how long, how high, and how deep his love really is*

(EPHESIANS 3:16-18 NLT).

# Journey Ministry

As with any journey, there are unseen detours, unexpected stops, surprising turns in the road—and priceless treasures to be found along the way. I want to encourage you and walk with you.

And no matter where the journey leads, God is there and He is more than enough!

*Mary*

**Mary Southerland** is a pastor's wife, the mother of two, an author, and an international speaker. A dynamic communicator, Mary delivers a powerful message that changes lives. She will make you laugh, cry, and walk away thirsting for more. Through warmth, humor, transparency, and solid biblical teaching, she leads women to discover the powerful truth of God's Word and motivates them to apply it in their daily lives. She is also the founder of Journey Ministry, a teaching ministry dedicated to equipping every woman for her unique journey to the heart of God.

Mary is available to speak for conferences, retreats, and women's events:

Web site: www.marysoutherland.com
E-mail: journeyfriends@cs.com
Phone: 704-843-2934

# Bible Credits

# Also by
# Mary Southerland

### SANDPAPER PEOPLE

Everybody deals with them—people who rub you the wrong way, often leaving abrasions behind! Mary goes beyond just giving good advice on how to handle tough relationships. You will see how God, using the difficult people in your life, is reshaping you into a person who can express His forgiveness, mercy, and tender affection.

### EXPERIENCING GOD'S POWER IN YOUR MINISTRY

Years of ministry have given Mary Southerland an influential platform from which to touch women serving God—whether through home and family, by leading a Bible study, via a staff position at church, or as a pastor's wife. *Experiencing God's Power in Your Ministry* distills key habits that will help you not just survive, but succeed.

### ESCAPING THE STRESS TRAP

"Stress management is a spiritual discipline," says Mary Southerland—a popular speaker who has found the keys to balancing writing, ministry, and a family life. In this thoughtful, creative, and helpful approach to dealing with life's stress, Mary looks at the Twenty-third Psalm as she inspires you to counter the culture's pressure to do it all on your own and to accept God's gift of stress-free living by trusting Him completely.

HARVEST HOUSE
PUBLISHERS